If we cannot do him honor
While he's here to hear the praise,
Then at least let's give him homage
At the end of his days.
Perhaps just a simple headline
In the paper that might say,
OUR COUNTRY IS IN MOURNING,
FOR A SOLDIER DIED TODAY.

— Author unknown

War Memories Are Forever!

Millie Jean Coppedge

EAKIN PRESS ✦ Fort Worth, Texas
www.EakinPress.com

This book was written in memory of my brother
Bruce Olen Coppedge, who died of cancer
on October 25, 1996, at the age of forty-six.

Its stories are dedicated to my five uncles who served
so gallantly and bravely in World War II.
William Hayward Reed was my grandmother's
firstborn son. The other four men were her brothers.

William Hayward Reed
Vestal Earle Palmer
J. W. Palmer
Billie Lee Palmer
Frank Palmer

Hayward and Frank did not return.

The first five stories are theirs.

Copyright © 2003
By Millie Jean Coppedge
Published By Eakin Press
An Imprint of Wild Horse Media Group
P.O. Box 331779
Fort Worth, Texas 76163
1-817-344-7036
www.EakinPress.com
ALL RIGHTS RESERVED
1 2 3 4 5 6 7 8 9
ISBN-10: 1-68179-087-4
ISBN-13: 978-1-68179-087-9

Contents

William Hayward Reed

U.S. Infantry
79th Division, 314 Regiment, 3rd Battalion,
Company K
Killed in Action

William Hayward Reed was the firstborn son of Lillie Mae and Alfred E. Reed of Coffeeville, Texas. Lillie Mae also saw her four brothers go to war. Her son and one brother did not return.

In order to get the complete picture of Hayward's story, some background must first be established. The inspiration for this book came when I viewed the fiftieth commemoration of the ending of World War II on a television special. As small children, my younger brother Bruce and I had walked the dirt road with Grandmother on a regular basis to visit Uncle Hayward's grave and clean it of weeds and debris. I remember Grandmother sitting on the ground as she smoothed the dirt and placed new artificial flowers near the headstone. Tears would roll down her cheeks, and the pain in her heart was most evident. But as a child of nine, I had no concept of the true magnitude of pain she held inside, that of losing her firstborn child.

For two years after my parents divorced, we lived with Grandmother and Granddaddy. I remember on several occasions, when everyone was gone except Grandmother and me, she would go into the back bedroom of her old frame house,

William Hayward Reed, killed in action, January 10, 1945.

gently unlock the deteriorating black trunk, and raise its lid. As she and I sat there on the plank floor, she would take out Uncle Hayward's personal belongings, touching each item, smelling them, trying to get back a sense of his being there. She would bury her face in some of his old clothes and sob, softly, but with a tone that was so heartbreaking. She had several packages of the letters he had written to her, each wrapped in what was once black ribbon but had faded to a faint color of dark purple. She would open the letters and hand one to me to read while she read another. I remember seeing the thick black lines through sentence after sentence, where the Army had censored things he had written. She would say, "He wrote us things he shouldn't have—things the government didn't want him to write home. We weren't supposed to know where he was fighting or what he was involved in."

Such a sad time for her. All four of her brothers and her son were in different parts of the world, fighting in the same war.

After the commemoration program was over that night, I vowed to try to find out more about Uncle Hayward's military service. Once I began to ask questions, the only living relatives who could possibly answer them were my mother and her brother. They knew very little, so I began with the information printed on his tombstone—his name, date of birth, date of death, and the division in which he served. I began writing letters to the camp where he took basic training, the War Department, the newspaper which printed that his body would be returned from New York, and the funeral home which took care of his final services in Gilmer, Texas, three years after his death. Each letter I received had several more suggestions and addresses to which I might write. Before long, I was in a writing campaign so involved that I had to buy a copying machine in order to make copies of incoming and outgoing letters. It would otherwise have been impossible to remember to whom and why I had written letters.

My first letter was mailed on December 11, 1994, and the research is still going on. Since Hayward is not here to tell his story, I will tell it for him, from the timeline that has taken me six years to put together.

Hayward was born on August 1, 1925. He was a farm boy

who spent most of his time in the fields. He had a brother, two sisters (one of whom is my mother), and three stepsisters. This family of nine was dirt-poor, struggling to survive from the soil. They grew every crop that the sandy East Texas dirt would produce. Hayward never had the time nor the inclination to date, so he died never having had a girlfriend. There was no time for girls or any type of social affairs, such as church socials, which were popular in those days.

On October 30, 1943, he received his induction notice from the Selective Service Board. By December 6, he was on his way to Camp Wolters, Texas. On January 4, 1944, he arrived at Camp Fannin, where he completed his basic training, but only after a second attempt. Halfway through the first training, he came down with a severe case of the big red measles, developed painful earaches with both ears draining, and had to be hospitalized for two weeks. After recuperating, he was instructed to begin basic training all over again.

By July 18, 1944, he was at Camp Van Dorn, Mississippi, and served his last time at Fort George G. Meade, Maryland. When I began my research on Uncle Hayward, the family thought that the only camp he had been in was Camp Fannin. They thought he went there for basic training, then was sent straight to war. That was how little contact they had with him during the war.

August 18, 1944, was his sailing date for Europe. Letters written to his mother, which were only found a little over a year ago in a rotting storeroom of her old home, told Lillie Mae on September 29, 1944, "Mother, I am somewhere in France." Servicemen were not allowed to tell the family back home exactly where they were. Their letters were censored very strictly.

What was to be Hayward's last letter arrived on October 25, 1944, asking his mother to send his French harp (harmonica). He said, "It gets very lonely in these foxholes, and if I can play my French harp, it will be a little like being at home."

His mother immediately sent the French harp, wrapped in a white cloth, snuggled in a box of her homemade cookies. Hayward never received the package. In December 1944, she received a telegram stating that he had been wounded. It seems that he had had several teeth shot out on December 12 but was put back on the front lines on the 14th. On January 9 another telegram came, informing them that he had been wounded again, and then came the final one, stating that he had died on January 10, 1945. He was nineteen years old.

The package of cookies containing the French harp wrapped with so much love, nestled in the homemade cookies, was returned unopened after his death. On February 21, 1945, Lillie Mae received a letter stating that two purple hearts were on the way, and on the 26th, one arrived from Carl A. Heckman, chaplin, U.S. Army, offering his condolences. The letter telling of his final resting place came on October 14, 1945. He was buried in Épinal, France, in a military cemetery.

The local newspaper, the *Gilmer Mirror*, published a lengthy article relating that Hayward's body had arrived in New York, brought from France on the USSAT *Robert F. Burns*. The next announcement was regarding the funeral, to be held on April 29, 1948. Hayward had finally been brought home to rest.

In conducting these years of research, men from Hayward's unit, the 79th Division, have related most of their tour route to me. Once in the eastern part of France, the infantrymen fought down the Moder River, through Bischeolts, Neubourg, Schweig-hausen, Hagenau (the Forest of Hagenau), on into Bischwiller, Drusenheim, Herrilsheim, and for Hayward, ended up in Rohrwiller.

Rohrwiller is near the Rhine River and is in the Black Forest. The weather was unbearably cold, and the men hadn't eaten for some time. As they approached a waterworks factory which generated electricity for the little town, they thought the factory was uninhabited. The Germans and the Americans had gone back and forth in the takeover of the factory, but the Americans thought it was empty. As they approached in the open field, the doors and windows were flung open and the Germans mowed most of the 79th Division down with machine guns, a bloody massacre in the white snow. Hayward was severely wounded, having been shot in the chest and right shoulder area. He was wounded on January 9, 1945, transferred to the 57th Field Hospital, and died the next day. He was buried, and three years later his body was shipped home for its final resting place.

The following poem which I wrote about Uncle Hayward was

read at the closing of the Proceeding and Debates Session of the 105th Congressional Session in the House of Representatives, Washington, D.C., by Representative Ralph Hall of Rockwall, Texas. Thus it is forever registered in the Congressional Records.

Hayward—A Tribute

Hayward, a farm boy in the heyday of his youth.
Up before the sun rose to light the aging wood heater.
The wind blew through the cracks in the walls.
The black tarpaper stretched to keep out the cold draft.
Oh, the aroma of Mama's country ham frying in the skillet.
Biscuits baking in the cookstove and coffee steaming in the
  blue granite pot.
Fluffy, country scrambled eggs with rich red-eye gravy.
Home-preserved muscadine jelly and fresh-churned creamy
  butter.
Hayward had not yet really tasted the adventures of life.
The farm work was hard and demanding.
There had been no time for girls or cars,
Country fairs, Sunday-afternoon rides, or church socials.
Then the call came from Uncle Sam's draft.
"We need you! It is your time to serve your country!"
He said good-bye to his loved ones and friends.
He hugged and kissed his mama for the last time.
A lump grew in his throat and tears welled in his eyes.
He tried to explain to his faithful old hound
That he would be away for a while.
Little did he know that he would never return.
The train ride to boot camp seemed like an endless journey.
The cropped haircut, strange clothes, fast-moving orders and
  expectations.
Bunking with boys who were forced to become men by a war
  they had not created.
Anticipating the adventure, yet lonesome for the warmth and
  smells of home.
Drills and marches, training for a fight beyond their
  imagination.
Finally, the order came.
Be ready to board the train for New York by morning.

The destination yet unknown to the men. France!
Off in the distance the shoreline of a strange new land.
Boats, tanks, movement, strategy.
Orders, guns, and tanks exploding.
The noise, the confusion, the panic of the moment.
Heavy boots, wool socks, sore aching, blistered feet.
The same clothes, worn day after day, lost their sophisticated
    military appeal.
He dug his own bed, a cold, damp foxhole.
When rain filled his haven, he used his helmet to dip it dry.
Penetrating deeper into the war-ravaged countryside.
The destruction his eyes beheld ripped at his gut, making him
    heave in horror.
Senseless slaughter of innocent people, young children, old
    women.
Made his heart weep, his eyes fill, and his body tremble.
A land once so beautiful, now lay smothered in total ruins.
A people rich in their culture, without a home.
All they ever knew and loved
Crumbled at the mercy of the enemy.
Marching into Rohrwiller, physically exhausted, emotionally
    drained.
No time for thoughts of tomorrow, every moment on constant
    guard.
Covering his buddies advancing to the front.
The chill of the darkness like a blanket spread over the city.
Then came the barrage like a blast from hell
From the water factory's many windows!
Mowing down the soldiers like hail in a rainstorm
Until the new-fallen snow reeked with the smell of blood.
The cries of pain and agony filled the night air
As one by one their breathing stopped.
Hayward lay mortally wounded.
In his dying breath, he whispered his final word, "Mother."
He will never see the brilliant sun rise over the tall pine trees
    in the pasture.
He will never celebrate another Christmas.
He will never know the joy of holding his firstborn child.
He will never hear his mother call his name again.

The United States of America

honors the memory of

William Hayward Reed

This certificate is awarded by a grateful nation in recognition of devoted and selfless consecration to the service of our country in the Armed Forces of the United States.

William J. Clinton

President of the United States

Vestal Earle Palmer

Staff Sergeant, 18th Battalion Infantry
Replacement Training Center, Company B
Second Wave to Land on Normandy Beaches
POW Stalag 3-C, near Berlin, Germany
POW Russian Concentration Camp

In the summer of 1998, I drove from Dallas to Abilene, Texas, in an attempt to visit Uncle Vestal, whom I had not seen in over thirty years, despite many letters, phone calls, and drop-by visits. As I drove up in front of his most dilapidated house, he was sitting in the front yard on a five-gallon can turned upside-down. I cautiously walked around the front of my car, not knowing what kind of a welcome to expect, and I was shocked when he stood with a delighted smile on his face.

"Uncle Vestal, I bet you don't know who I am," I said, coming to a standstill at the edge of the sidewalk.

"Why, Millie Jean. Of course I know who you are. You're Lizzie Mae's daughter. Come on up here!"

He gave me a big hug and offered an unbelievably dirty plastic chair to sit in. No other family member had seen him since about 1975. Vestal had become a recluse and had cut off all ties with all family members. For over three and a half hours we talked. I told him that I had come to interview him for the book I was writing, and asked him if he would give me his story or some of his war experiences and allow them to be published.

9

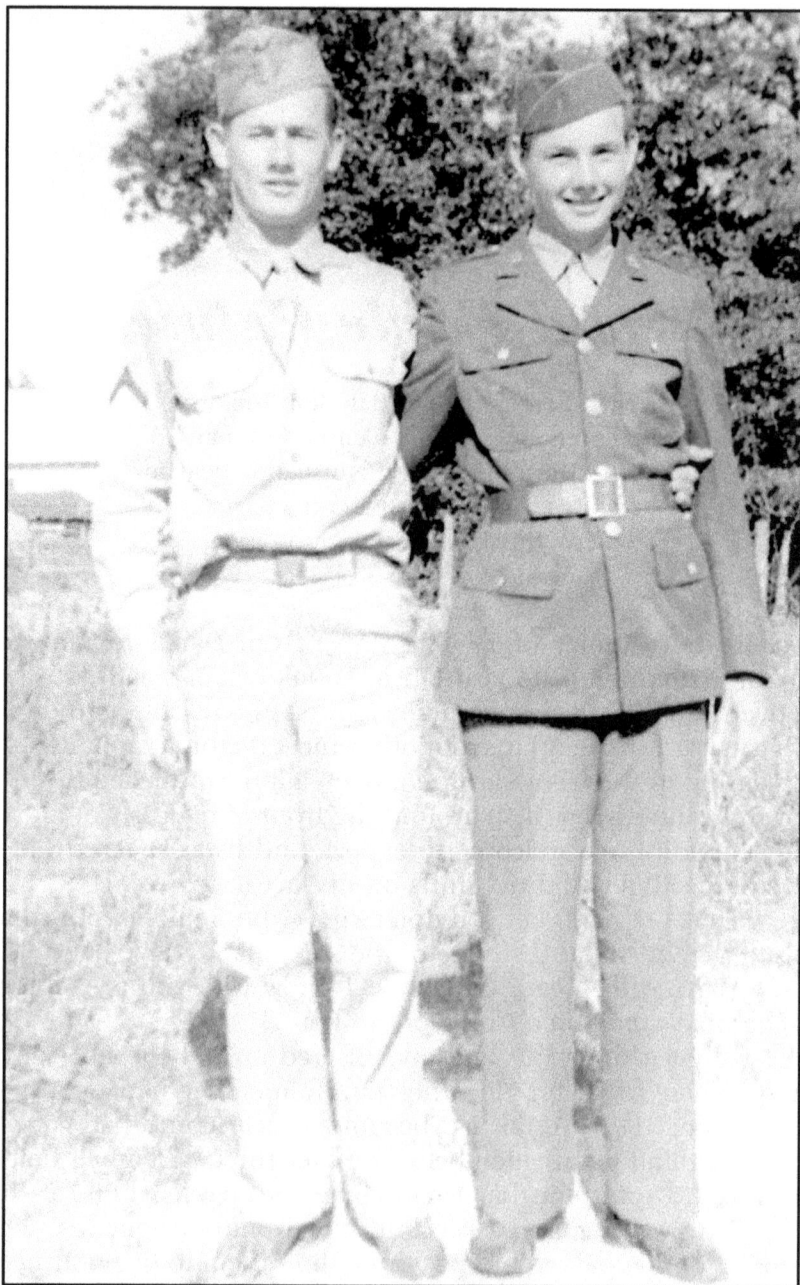

Vestal Earl Palmer (left) with nephew William Hayward Reed,
approximately 1944.

He began talking, covering not only the war, but his youth, heartaches, adventures, struggles with the government, and disagreements with family members. The tale he wove was so intertwined, it was often difficult to follow him. He relived being one of ten children born to a poor farming family. He laughed and blushed a little when he told how he was nursed by a black woman called "Auntie." It seems that his mother did not have enough breast milk to accommodate both his twin sister and him, so the woman down the road agreed to breast-feed him, since she had enough milk for her newborn and him, too.

His striking steel blue eyes sparkled as he talked about being raised in Buckner's Orphans Home in Dallas. He was valedictorian of his graduating class at "The Home," and had many fond memories of playing football and roller-skating. Shortly after the warm smiles came a painful sadness, as he related his war experiences. The following is his story:

I was born On August 15, 1922. My name is Vestal Earl and my twin sister was Vera Merle. My mother gave birth to ten children but three died in childhood—one at birth, one of diphtheria, and the other at age three of unknown causes. When my baby sister Katherine was only three months old, Mother died of tuberculosis. Eight months later, Daddy was gored to death in the back yard by a bull. Both of my parents were only in their early thirties when they died.

Our oldest brothers, Frank and Bill, took care of us for two years, until they could no longer care for us all. The four youngest, Catherine, almost three, Vera and I, age four, and J. W., age six, were sent to Buckner's Orphan's Home. J. W. left the home once he was of age, while Vera, Catherine, and I continued to live there until we graduated.

On October 17, 1942, I was drafted into the Army. After basic training, I was sent as a replacement to England. After crossing the English Channel, we were the second wave to land on the beaches of Normandy, France. My unit spent fifty days in Normandy.

Once I was in a foxhole with heavy mortar fire coming in. I had a full cup of hot coffee in my hand, trying to get warm. A bullet shattered the cup and the scalding coffee went all over me, but I wasn't hurt at all.

I served at Crentan, was at St. Lo, which fell on July 19, 1944, and at the Urie River, which was bombed twice. Around this time, I received heavy shrapnel in the back.

On July 31, 1944, I was shot in the back, captured by the Germans, and sent to Stalag-3C concentration camp near Berlin, Germany. I stayed there for six months. My family was informed that I was Missing in Action.

At one point, I hadn't had anything to eat in days. We only got about a quarter of the Red Cross parcels, and the Germans were very poor. They could barely feed themselves, much less us. I was so hungry that I traded my beloved high school graduation ring to a German Soldier for a tiny piece of hard German bread made from sawdust. When you're hungry, you'll do anything you have to do. You'll eat anything. We ate insects and rodents. But going without water was the hardest thing. We were eating one day and one of my buddies asked me for my church key. You know, a can opener. He wanted to open a can of meat and he had lost his. Mine was on my dog tags on a chain around my neck, so I took it off a let him use it. The next thing we knew, all hell broke loose, and the Germans started yelling for us to run into the woods. We could hear tanks and artillery approaching.

That's how I got wounded again. As we fled into the woods behind Stalag 3-C, the Russians didn't know if we were Germans or POWs, or what, so they started shootin' at us. I got hit in the ankle and in the arm. I fell to the ground and played dead. The Russian platoon sergeant thought I was dead, so they left me. After four days of hiding out in the woods, the Russians captured me. I wouldn't talk. Since I didn't have my dog tags, they didn't know if I was German, American, or who the hell I was.

They tried to torture and starve it out of me. I went days and days without food or water. It's a lot easier to go without food than it is water. When I still wouldn't talk, they took me outside and lined me up with fifteen other men. They put me in the middle. When I still wouldn't talk, they started shootin' the men in the head, killing them one by one. When they got to me, they once again asked me to talk. Dripping with the men's blood and brain matter, I still refused to speak. So they continued killing the men, until they were all dead. It was a tough decision to make. But I knew they would kill us all anyway, and if I could survive somehow, maybe I could live to tell what happened. It was a horrible thing, and it's on my mind every day of my life, and I'll die with it on my mind.

• • •

After the war, Vestal graduated from North Texas College with a bachelor's degree in business administration. He worked for an insurance company as a IBM operator, then eight years with the Internal Revenue Service, and finally went into business for himself completing businesses' and individuals' income taxes.

Vestal Earl Palmer, 1999.

Vestal's decorations included an EAMET Service Medal, a Good Conduct Medal, three Silver Stars, and four Purple Hearts.

Vestal was found on a cold Wednesday morning, February 9, 2000, about 8:00 A.M., lying dead in his front yard on a thin mattress rotten with filth. He was covered with a shirtwaist coat, and his baseball cap covered his face. He had slept outside for years. After his death, it became apparent that he had also spent a lot of time under his house, as a hole was discovered in a bedroom closet, and blankets and lanterns lay beside a comfy nest in the soft, sandy dirt, obviously where he had lain on many occasions.

Approximately the last twenty years of his life, he had become a paranoid schizophrenic, enduring most of his days reliving the war. For him, time had stood still. It was still 1942.

He died as he would probably have preferred it, alone. I wonder—just what was the last thing on his mind?

J. W. Palmer, approximately 1944.

J. W. Palmer

United States Army
Rank and unit unknown

J. W. Palmer was ten years older than his brother, Vestal. He entered the service in March 1942. His tour began in Australia, New Guinea, then went on to include Leyte and Bataan, Philippines, and in Mendora, Japan. He served under Gen. Douglas MacArthur. He was in a Japanese concentration camp, having endured inhumane torture.

On June 22, 1945, during the invasion of Devow City in the Philippines, he was shot and received numerous serious skin abrasions and bruises, and was evacuated to Leyte, Philippines. Later he was transported back to the states, where he spent four months recuperating in the VA Hospital. He retired from the service in 1964.

His service decorations included the Asiatic-Pacific Theater Medal with three Bronze Stars, Philippines Liberation Ribbon with two Bronze stars, Good Conduct Medal, Silver Star, three Bronze Arrows, and a Purple Heart.

J. W. married a Japanese woman, then returned after the war to serve a tour of duty in Japan. They had no children. His wife preceded him in death. He died on her birthday, September 1, 1998.

Vestal and Billie Palmer.

Billie Lee Palmer

United States Army
Rank and unit unknown

Bill Palmer was drafted into the Army. He served four months on the battlefront and was then sent home at the war's end, as all the servicemen were. This is all that is known about his service.

Frank Palmer, age eighteen.

Frank Palmer

Possibly Merchant Marines
Rank and unit unknown

Frank was the oldest of the brothers. He was either in the Coast Guard or the Navy. Probably the Merchant Marines, as was told by the now deceased brother, J. W. Palmer.

He was on a freighter loaded with oil headed for North Africa. The tanker disappeared and was never heard from again. It was assumed that the Japanese torpedoed the ship. The name of the ship is also unknown.

The family had not heard from Frank for years before the war, as he, too, had become a loner, like Vestal. The only way they knew he had been reported missing was when his life insurance policy was paid to Vestal.

Lillie Mae, his sister, had hoped up until the day she died that someday Frank would walk up onto her front porch and knock at the door. She prayed that, rather than going down with the ship, he had been captured by the enemy and had been in a POW camp all those years. But he never came home.

Herman H. Edwards, taken at Dachau Train Station, April 1945.

Herman H. Edwards

257th Engineer Combat Battalion
European Theater of Operations, 1944–45

I was born in Dickenson County, Virginia, on August 3, 1925, and lived on a farm until I was drafted into the military service in August 1943. I completed basic training as a combat medic at Camp Gordon, Georgia, near Augusta. The cadre that was responsible for our training was made up of regular Army and was at Pearl Harbor when it was bombed. Needless to say, they were very aggressive during our training. The 257th Engineer Combat Battalion consisted of men from Pennsylvania, New York, and Virginia, and one fellow from a ranch in Oklahoma.

Our battalion departed from England on October 30, 1944, and arrived on November 10, 1944. We left England after a month's special training and landed at Cherbourg, France. Then we proceeded to Normandy, St. Lo, Paris, and on into Germany. We were responsible for 1,100 square miles throughout this area, where we experienced one of the most severe winters in over a decade. Due to improper footwear, we encountered considerable difficulty with frost boils and trenchfoot. I avoided this problem by changing my socks frequently and carried several pairs in my helmet and under my shirt. I firmly believe that if I had not had the farm experience, which had kept me in good physical shape, and with God's help, I would have had difficulty surviving.

The war ended May 7, 1945, and soon after the battalion was disbanded and was on their way into the Army occupation with the 126th Engineer Combat Battalion and was discharged on May 7, 1946.

The GI Bill allowed me to enroll in college in September 1946. I completed my degree at Tennessee Wesleyan College in Athens, Tennessee, and Tennessee Tech University, Cookeville, Tennessee, in January 1950. Following graduation, I was employed by Burroughs Corporation in Detroit, Michigan, and retired in 1986 as a senior industrial engineer in Mission Viejo, California.

The one thing I do believe is that the Second World War was a moral and just war, to rid the world of a dictator who caused many deaths and much suffering. Tom Brokaw's book *The Greatest Generation* gave many examples regarding the attitude and ingenuity of the Citizen Soldier in achieving victory in Europe and the Pacific. These soldiers came from farms, ranches, and factories and had strong work ethics. This was displayed during the D-Day Invasion at Omaha, Utah, and other areas of conflict where there was utter confusion under fire. Faced with the impossible, it was the soldiers' ingenuity that made them superior over their enemy and enabled them to achieve the victory.

• • •

The above is Edward's tour in a nutshell as he relates it. But the 257th Engineer Combat Battalion was trained in the construction and maintenance of roads and bridges, guarding military installations, removing roadblocks, filling bomb craters, and the most dangerous job of locating and destroying mines and booby traps. His battalion received a special commendation from Maj. Vincent J. Bellis for building "the fourth floating bridge ever to be constructed across the Rhine River, and the third ever to be build in wartime."

The following account of the events that happened at Dachau Concentration Camp was submitted by Edwards to be used as part of his story.

Dachau Concentration Camp

The following excerpt is taken from the end of a story of a lengthy, detailed, day-by-day document of the wartime experiences of a soldier in the 257th Engineer Combat Battalion. It was written to a soldier's sweetheart, dated June 5, 1945. Although Mr. Edwards sent a copy of the entire story to his parents in 1945, he can't remember the soldier's name. The story begins with "Hello Darling" and simply ends with "so long, be seeing you."

This section of the story begins toward the end of his account:

When we first entered the town, we questioned a couple of men we saw walking in striped uniforms. We learned those were the uniforms of Dachau. They told us that the whole camp was full of dead bodies that the Germans had murdered last week. They said that the figure would run into at least ten thousand. They told us of how every day someone would be murdered in cold blood, as a warning to the other inmates that they were the slaves and the Germans, the masters. The men looked half starved and one of them had a pronounced tubercular cough.

These men took off their uniform jackets and, baring their backs, showed us the half-healed welts from the torturer's whip. We had heard enough to put us into a black rage. But again, we reasoned this could not be, this town doesn't look like it could foster such a Frankenstein. For as yet, we hadn't seen with our own eyes. We only had the words of persons who had been there, and we figured that they would naturally exaggerate, so as to gain sympathy for themselves. They were trying to bum cigarettes from us, but we were hurting ourselves and could only give them a few.

We moved on then with our billets. And soon after this, we had our orders to take over the guarding of the camp. Now, at least, we would have an opportunity to see these things that so many people had told us about.

Our first glimpse of the camp was from a wide road that encircled it, taking us past the SS officers' barracks and a great gate having an enormous German Eagle on top of a swastika. Then, coming to the main entrance, we were passed by our guards at the gate and started posting our guards at all the entrances and exits from the grounds. The object was to keep the inmates from roaming the streets and to prevent any SS men who had taken refuge in the hospital from also making their getaway.

The next morning, I went on a little reconnaissance, and coming to a high wall, walked along it until I found a gate. Entering this, the first thing to greet my eyes were the dog kennels, which housed the vicious dogs that they used to torture these poor unfortunate people. The Germans would strip the prisoners nude, then hanging them up by their thumbs so that their toes barely touched the floor, would let the dogs into the pen that the prisoners were in. The dogs, having been fed nothing but raw meats and having been trained to just such work, would wait on the keeper's next move, which would usually be to touch the prisoners on their private parts with a stick. The dogs, at this command, would jump up and attempt to bite at the object touched by the stick. In my mind, this was not only inhumane, but a sure sign of degenerate, sadistic, psychopathic tendencies.

The dogs by now had all been killed by the American soldiers who had taken over the town, but some of the brutes were still lying in their kennels. They were the largest, most vicious-looking animals I had ever seen in my whole life.

From the kennel area, I came to a path and, turning into it, came to another large gate which opened into a yard. At first, I didn't notice what was directly in front of my eyes.

But suddenly, it dawned on me what I was looking at. There, no more than fifty yards away, was a huge pile of nude, partly decomposed bodies. I had stumbled on the Charnel House of the Devil himself, the crematorium that we had heard so much about but actually doubted the existence of. The bodies were stacked like so much cordwood and had been dumped there in anticipation of being burned the following day. But the butchers had been interrupted in their work by the arrival of our troops. There must have been at least 300 bodies in that one stack alone. To go further into the description of this sight and the stench of decomposition and death that hung over the piles of bodies would not only turn your stomach, but I am afraid it would give me the screaming meeemies, AGAIN. Walking past the pile, I entered the crematorium itself, but just entering the door was enough. The stench here was enough to floor a person, and all the rooms were full of dead bodies in every state of decomposition, having been liberally sprinkled with lime.

I felt my marbles slowly starting to come up, so I left there with as much speed as possible. Never will I forget that sight, nor the awful smell that surrounded the place. All of those people had either been shot through the head unmercifully or bashed in the head sadistically, or had been torturously starved to death. The majority of those dead were either Poles, Russians, or Jews.

The Germans who were at this camp, and the political prisoners from other countries such as Holland, France, or Norway, were treated as well as could be expected under the circumstances. That is, as long as they worked at the job assigned to them. If they attempted to evade working, they were whipped the same as the others and put on shorter rations than usual, which according to our standards, are less than starvation rations. In talking to them, we learned more about how the Russians and Jews had been treated.

A Hollander told us of a incident that had happened two days before our arrival. He spoke of 350 women having been marched 200 miles from another camp that had been threatened by our troops. Immediately after their arrival, they were fed and bedded down. In the morning, they were told to march over to an assigned area and to remove their clothes. There they were told they would be given new clothing. Having done this as ordered, the women were marched into the crematorium, unknowingly, and were burned alive.

I know this sounds incredible in the telling of it. That it seems impossible that they would go to so much trouble. But it was all to impress the other prisoners of how little they should value their lives.

The camp had been under quarantine because of a fear on our medics' part that the typhus then so rampant through the camp would spread into an epidemic. Anyone entering had to be dusted with a delousing powder, and no one other than authorized persons were allowed to leave. We were inoculated that same day. At that time, I took our medical officer over to see the bodies. By now, the macabre pile had become famous, and people from every country were gathering evidence against the Germans and were there checking figures and facts concerning the deaths. There were reporters, photographers, artists, diplomats, and high-ranking officers of every country in Europe.

As we entered the yard, an Air Force officer, who was taking motion pictures of the assemblage and bodies, came over to us and asked us to pose near the unholy mess. We agreed and he took about four pictures of us, saying that he wanted to show the people back home how we felt about it. He mentioned the fact that he didn't think we would have to do any acting. And boy, he was right! We got up to within two feet of the bodies, and here the stench hit us in the face like a sledgehammer!

Disgust, nausea, and vivid hatred for the people who had perpetrated such a crime were all mirrored in our faces. I was very glad that he was competent and didn't take any longer than necessary, for even though I'd seen them the day before, I still couldn't stand the smell or the sight. My stomach was doing flip-flops.

Up to now, they were trying to burn the bodies, but each day they would find more, and the concentration area of the camp would yield about a hundred or more deaths a day from those who were so far gone in the stages of malnutrition that nothing else could be done to save them. Naturally, this over-taxed the facilities at the crematorium, so they decided to dig a common grave on the outskirts of town and load the bodies into carts and take them through town to bury them. I thought this was a capital idea, for I wanted to see the reaction of the people of Dachau when they saw the results of the fiendish regime that they had fostered and hailed for the past ten years.

As the carts slowly filed through town with their grisly cargo, the people stared at them with handkerchiefs held to their noses. If they saw an American looking at them, they would shrug their shoulders as though to say, "I had nothing to do with this. This is the work of the Nazis. I was never a Nazi, never did I know what was going on." And they actually had the effrontery to think that we were ignorant enough to believe that they didn't know such a thing existed in their city. I heard another girl say, "It is a shame to be a German." She was right. The Germans have more to repay than they can ever atone for. And if the combined military governments do not do something about it, then may God have mercy on their souls, for they will have failed dismally in the completion of the task for which thousands of our American boys gave up their lives.

Every day for a week, seven to ten cartloads of bodies would pass by on their way to the common burial ground. Still, the town's people denied having any knowledge of such a condition existing. They admitted that they knew about the camp, but they were adamant in their denial of being cognizant of the torture and deaths that were a daily part of Camp Dachau.

The prisoners had a bit of a field day when our tanks appeared at the camp's gate. They immediately turned on their craven guards, and evidence of their prowess was to be found in the dead bodies' grotesque positions. They were cruelly beaten, and in some cases were left for dead but didn't die until hours later, for signs of their death struggles could be seen in the scuffed ground around the bodies.

Some of the bigshots of the camp were taken prisoner in the town. They were found living in homes as respected citizens, having threatened the tenants of the house with death and worse if they gave them up. But the people in the homes that the SS had hidden in feared the American authorities more, and succeeded in letting us know where we could pick up these fiends. When captured, they were taken back to the scene of their crime and given a chance to confess to some of the atrocities that they had committed. But the Germans were a hard lot, and no amount of persuasion, either harsh or gentle, would sway them in their determination not to talk. They knew they would be shot whether they talked or not, so they decided that the less said, the better off they would be.

But one of our boys decided this issue for them. Having gotten just a little tight, and having come from seeing the bodies in the crematorium, he had heard about the authorities having this officer in custody. So he was inquisitive to see just what kind of a toad this guy was. Coming into the room where he and his assistants were sitting in glowering silence, neither answering his questions nor looking from right to left, but just straight ahead, made this boy just mad enough to want to do something about it. He asked for permission to try to make them talk.

Having been granted this permission, he walked over to the German officer, who was wearing glasses at the time. Drawing back his fist, the boy whacked the German a beauty right smack on the nose, sending his glasses spinning. Then the boy ground them into the floor, and proceeded to work out on the German louse's nose, hitting him there in the exact same spot about a dozen times. This was too much for the man, and asking for mercy, he agreed to write. Reluctantly, this outraged American youth desisted and was disappointed when the others followed their leader's action rather than go through what he had experienced.

The name Dachau will long remain in the memories of the world. To perpetuate this name as synonymous with all that is horrible in the annals of Nazism, its name should be changed to "Death."

When peace was announced on May 8, none of us could celebrate it or feel much emotion over the event that we had wished for and prayed for, month after monotonous, death-laden month. We had all been emotionally washed out. It was impossible to feel cheerful in a town so full of horror and grief.

• • •

This was the end of the soldier's story.

Herman Edwards served in the 126th Engineer Combat Battalion and helped liberate the Dachau Concentration Camp. He was going to write his experiences of the liberation, but sent their soldier's story instead, saying that he could not write it better, noting the emotional sensitivity with which the author describes a most horrendous, unthinkable atrocity done to our fellow man.

Herman H. Edwards, 1999

Joe W. Campbell

79th Infantry Division,
314th Regiment, 2nd Battalion

To preface this experience. I was a wireman in the 314th Regimental Headquarters Company of the 79th Division. Our primary duty was to maintain telephone communications between the regimental command post and the three battalion headquarters company command posts. This was done by laying telephone wire from reels on a jeep on the ground, mainly, and repairing the wire when it was broken by whatever means, and there were many. Restoration ASAP was imperative. To accomplish this, crews were located at a suitable place somewhere between the regimental CP area and the battalion CPs. This reduced the time considerably, as well as to reduce the amount of exposure to enemy fire.

On January 5, 1945, the 314th Regiment moved to the vicinity of Bischwiller, France, Alsace. The next two weeks were spent in an area that included Rohrwiller and Drusenheim, as well as several other smaller towns and villages on or near the Rhine River. The Germans were relieved of Rohrwiller on January 6. Rohrwiller was approximately two miles east of Bischwiller and two miles west of Drusenheim. The three towns were on a somewhat straight line west to east of Rohrwiller in the middle and slightly south of the straight line. After Rohrwiller was taken, my crew was moved there from Bischwiller to maintain telephone service from Rohrwiller to Drusenheim, part of

Joe W. Campbell, October 21, 1943, Muskogee, Oklahoma.

which was occupied by the 2nd Battalion midafternoon of the same day. This joint occupancy with the Jerries was to continue for the next two weeks. Invariably, as we got within a few hundred yards of Drusenheim from or behind the woods known as B. de Drusenheim, which was on the right side of the road with a cleared field approximately 300 yards wide between the road and the woods, we drew artillery or mortar fire. We hit that spot with a speed that would get us to the first house on the right as soon as possible. One of the other crews got two flat tires on their jeep just as they reached the house. It was determined it might be safer for us if we approached the town from the north instead of from the west, so we moved from Rohrwiller to Schirrhein, which was approximately two miles north from Drusenheim. This did not eliminate the enemy fire, but it did reduce it somewhat and it came from a different direction. This time it came from the left side of the road with another open field and then woods.

Early afternoon of January 19, it came my time to go repair the line which had been laid between our new location and Drusenheim. John "Pop" Mravinac, the jeep driver, and I headed out. A crew consisted of a jeep and five wiremen when at full force. It did not take long to figure out that for most of the times , two could do the job, so we could take turns in going in pairs, which reduced the risk and danger chances by about half. The line had been laid on the ground alongside the road to the first house on the left at Drusenheim, in front of the house across the small yard and over the railroad tracks that ran north-south somewhat parallel to the road. Then it went left at a 90-degree turn, up the gravel road for about 100 yards to a large wooden building something like a barn, making a 90-degree right hand turn around the corner of the building on a battalion, but I do not know how far because that was as far as I had ever been that way.

The line had been laid by hand across the yard and railroad because the tracks were too high for the jeep to drive across. When I got out of the jeep to trace the line by holding it in my cupped hand so I could feel the break or damage, I told Pop to go down to the end of the road, which ended at the point it reached the Rohrwiller-Drusenheim road, turn left, cross the railroad and turn left onto the road that came up alongside the railroad, and I would meet him across from the house.

About the time I got across the tracks, I saw Pop going up the next street over. I could just see the upper part of him and the top of the jeep through the wrought-iron fence that was on top of the cemetery wall. That was the last time I ever saw Pop. He had gone one street too far after crossing the railroad.

With the line in my hand, I started up the road toward the wooden building. In addition to holding the line in my hand for "feel," I looked for the damaged area and approached the building. I looked up and saw two wiremen from 2nd Battalion completing the repair of the break in the line. I asked them if they knew Pop Kravniac and they said they did. I asked them to tell him to pick me up at the house where he let me out and they said they would.

I turned and had not taken a dozen steps when the enemy shells hit the far end of the railroad station, which was almost directly across from the house. I made a fast beeline to the open door and left down the stairs which were just inside the door. Needless to say, the railroad was out of operation and the station was not manned, at least with railroad personnel. It was dark in the basement, and I could hear people talking in a language I could not understand. Most likely, French civilians. Anyway, out of there I got about as fast as in I went, crossed the railroad and got in the basement of the house, which did not seem to have any furniture in it, although I did not explore the place.

We probably got to the house on the way in about 1:00 or 2:00 P.M. and by this time it was probably around 3:00, but it already seemed like I had been there all day. We were not supposed to have anything on our person that would help the enemy in any way. The only thing I had was a picture of a girlfriend in my cigarette case. I took it out and threw it on the floor and after further thought, picked it up. Even to this day, I can see that picture lying on the floor. Minutes passed as hours, and that is all that passed. Not one soldier or one vehicle for the next couple of hours. I had no hope whatsoever as to getting out of there. Darkness was setting in and it was about 5:30 P.M.. I was standing out in the ward at the gate, and all of a sudden in came a jeep roaring down the road from Schirrhein. They saw me and stopped. It was one of the I&R (Intelligence and Reconnaissance) teams from my company, that had come to see what was going on and what the situation was. As the next few minutes revealed, it did not take them long to find out. I asked them if they were coming back and they said they were.

"Will you pick me up?" I asked.

"Yes." they replied.

It probably was not more than 300 yards to the intersection. All hell had broken loose, probably half a mile south of there, along the railroad tracks. Coming north up along the railroad was any kind of fire you can think of except bombs—tank, mortar, artillery, small arms, etc. Then that jeep came back up the road in four-wheel drive, roaring like a tank. One of the guys was standing up with his hands on the handle of the machine, ready to fire at whatever moved. They had found out firsthand what was going on and what the situation was, and it was not good. They had shrapnel in the jeep to prove it, and luckily no one was wounded. By this time it was dark, and I was fearful they would not stop, but they did. As we tore up the road, all kinds of fire was streaming parallel to the road and about fifty yards to the left. The open fields were flat and the road made lazy S's across them with trees on both sides, with quite a display of tracers. I am sure those curves were not as curvy as they were before the driver took some curve out of them. We safely escaped!

By 5:00 A.M., January 20, the Germans completed the captivity of the 2nd Battalion except for about 240 officers and enlisted men. I guess the Germans knew how many prisoners they had that morning, but certainly no one in the 314th knew. For one reason, the battalion was severely undermanned. No doubt they took more GIs than were not taken.

I never saw Pop again and we never made contact. I learned that he survived got back to Chicago and married Mary, his girlfriend. We had heard that his jeep was hit and received two flat tires and he stayed in the basement of a house until he was captured. In 1993, John Q. Aven of Calhoun City, Missouri, who was in the same group of prisoners, told me he kidded Pop about the reason he let the Germans capture him was that he was afraid to let Capt. Fred Rogers, who was in charge of our communications group, know that he had four flat tires on the jeep. Guess that is the reason he did not meet me back over at the house. He told me Pop had died a few years prior to 1993. Aven was in one of the other I & R teams and was captured in Drusenheim.

I went back in 1993, and the railroad still runs through Drusenheim, and the station is still there but out of use. That little brick house is gone, for what reason I do not know. I stood on the station platform and looked down the road and could see the Rohrwiller-Drusenheim road where Pop turned but failed to take a left on the gravel road.

Only God knows why Pop instead of me, and why not me in the place of one of those hundreds of thousands.

Story 2

One of the initial memories that has lived with me all these years was on the morning of June 14, 1944. The six-by-six trucks had picked us up at the concentration area on the southern coast of England near Southampton, where we had received our last supper, which consisted of English mutton, carrots, and peas, and also our last breakfast. I was sitting on one side of the truck at the back, and Lieutenant Kerns was sitting opposite me on the other side. It was very crowded and uncomfortable with all the gear, clothing, and ammunition we had on.

As we were approaching the area where we would unload and get on the vessel that would take us across the English Channel, I had to make some adjustment to the ammunition that was heavy and bulky, attached to my ammunition belt. I just unbuttoned the flap on my gas mask and put the hand grenades in there. I thought nothing about it but later learned from some of the guys that had been in the outfit a lot longer than I that they were shocked to see me do what I did right in the face of Lieutenant Kerns. That was a "no-no" that they had learned the hard way months ago in basic training. A soldier was to put nothing in the gas mask—it was to be ready for immediate use at all times. A very minor incident in the face of the greatest invasion effort mankind had ever known or will ever know. But with the danger of combat only hours and a few watery miles away, even though he did not say a word, I am sure Lieutenant

Kerns and I were on the same wavelength. This was war, and a soldier does what he has to do.

We reached Utah Beach late that afternoon and climbed down the rope nets into the LCIs (Landing Craft Infantry), for the final short leg of the journey from that golf-course camp near Manchester, England, to the sandy, bloody, battle-scarred beach of France. We started the six-mile journey up and over the sand dunes, over the narrow path that the engineers had cleared and marked through the minefield. An advance party of a few men from our company had preceded us by a couple of days. After we had trudged a mile or so under the full complement of equipment assigned to a soldier entering uninvited enemy territory to obtain an invasion foothold, we looked up and there went George Bowyer, a six-by-six truck driver from our company. He was headed up the beach to pick up supplies. His mission accomplished, he picked some of us up, as many as could get on the truck, on his way back. Man! Were we glad to see him! That ride sure neutralized, what seemed like hundreds of pounds of weight consisting of two layers of clothing, jacket, full field pack, gas mask, ammunition, rifle, and other necessary articles that a combat soldier needed and could carry.

The Regimental Headquarters Company area the advance party had picked was near Blosville, and we reached it about 7:00 P.M. The very first thing was to dig a foxhole. I picked out a spot and started immediately. The corporal of the guard, Rex Spratlin, a six-foot-plus young kid from Mississippi, came over to me and said they wanted me to go over and help dig the officers' slit trench, or outdoor toilet. I told him, "No way until I got my foxhole dug!"

He did not say anything, just walked off. He came back a little later and said he had guard duty at midnight and he would dig in my place if I would do his guard duty. I told him I would because I would have my foxhole dug by then. Rex had been in the advance party and he had a foxhole already dug.

I will never forget the first night in France. My post was on the other side of the hedgerow that bordered the field the advance party had picked for the company's C (Command Post). I had to walk back and forth between two corners of the hedgerow. The night was so black and dark that I could not even see myself. I knew a German could sneak up and cut my throat and I would never know what had happened. I was so scared that a nail could not have been driven between my teeth with a ten-pound sledgehammer.

Then all hell broke loose! The Germans sent a plane over to see what was going on at the beach. From the sound, I could tell it was flying real low. All of a sudden, the sky lit up with anti-aircraft—ack-ack and machine gun fire. The dead silence of the night was shattered by explosive firing of the guns and the constant stream of bullets slicing the air on the way toward that Jerry plane. The tracer bullets painted a picture of bright red ropes strung out across the sky in a pattern that cannot be described. I would be surprised if that Jerry survived. Thank God this scared GI did!

This memory is just as fixed in my being as is my heartbeat and my breathing. It was nothing I did just what I experienced as a nineteen-year-old kid from Tennessee that had never been 100 miles from home until my Uncle Sam pointed his finger to me and said, "I want you!"

Looking back, I realize they would have made an example out of me with a court martial, but at the moment I did not give that a thought. I just could not see digging a trench for officers to relieve themselves when I did not have a hole to put my butt in.

Story 3

By midmorning of November 29, 1944, 2nd Battalion, 314th Infantry Regiment, 79th Division had taken Nieder-schaeffolsheim. Sometime after that, probably the 30th or December 1, our crew, led by Cpl. Sam Barnett of Englewood, Tennessee, set up a switchboard in that town that had every evidence it had been surrendered, and it had been taken only after every effort possible had been expended in the transfer. It was a mess! Even so, we found a house that had survived and was suitable for our needs. It was a multi-structure. Standing in the street facing the building on the left and just a few feet back from the street was what I would call a beer parlor/dance hall and was approximately twenty-five to thirty feet square and rather nice for such a small town. Behind that area and attached were four rooms that served as the living quarters, one of which was used to locate our switchboard. On the right-hand side, and a little farther back from the street than the dance hall, was a barn-like section that had a large opening in the front end that would clear a six-by-six truck. Connecting the two was a center section divided into storage rooms, stalls, etc. It was in the shape of a rough U, designed to provide a social gathering place, living quarters for a family, and accommodate chickens and a few animals with a small courtyard in front. The center section was not as high as the two end sections. There was a deep, full-size basement under the dance hall section.

We had been there a couple of days when Sam told me there were several elderly men and women staying in the basement. I went over and opened the door at the head of the stairs and could not believe what I saw. In the dimly lit basement were probably twenty-plus men and women that could have been in their seventies or eighties. No doubt they considered it the safest place in town. To my knowledge, none of our crew communicated with them. Later that morning, they all labored up that steep set of steps and left. A few hours later, we heard an explosion that seemed to be just outside the window of the room in which the switchboard was located, but the glass did not break.

One of the battalion or line companies had set up their portable kitchens in the barn section, just outside the big opening. We ran outside to see what was going on and saw that the building was on fire. It became so engulfed in flames, no doubt from the dry straw, hay, etc., so fast that we could not get any of the equipment or belongings out, including the switchboard. All we had left was what we stored in the wooden ammunition box strapped to the hood of the jeep, just in front of the windshield, such as writing paper, cigarette, toilet articles, etc.

Before we moved on from Niederschaeffolsheim, we went back to the burned-out building for one last look. We noticed that one of the galvanized cans from that company kitchen, used to heat water for washing mess kits in, had very small holes in the side near the bottom, at such angles that it appeared they had been made from the ground upward. A land mine could have been involved, because it was evident the Germans had used the

building from hand grenades and other ammunition they had
left in the loft of the center section of the building we had seen.
We did not know where the fire started, if it caused the explosion
we had heard, or if the explosion had caused the fire. Perhaps incoming artillery. It would have been awfully hard to accept sabo-
tage from the occupants of the basement. Why they left and
where they went, we did not know. It really did not matter! You
were out with your life and the last second was history. Your only
concern was the future of your next breath. Not the history of the
last or what had happened. And whatever happens next would be
history with your next breath. Not every moment of a combat soldier's life is a death threat, but over a short period of time, the
threats are so frequent and constant that such is the mental mold
and attitude a soldier just naturally develops. Self-preservation,
not history and details, is the consuming force!

Story 4

Fraimbois, France, is a small, rural, dirt-road village. On
September 21, 1944, our company moved its CP forward to that
place. The wire crew that I was a member of picked a house on
the right-hand side of the road as you go north toward Foret de
Parroy for our shelter. It was one of those typical French houses
with an attached section at the back for storage, etc., other than
for an area in which to live. That was the part of the house that
we chose for our sleeping quarters. Adjacent to that part of the
building was a small outside chicken lot containing several
chickens. From appearances, the house was occupied but no one
was home. We had found just what we needed. In a couple hours
it would be suppertime, so why not? Sam Barnette, our wire crew
chief, went to the lot and came back with two chickens. Cleaned,
killed, and cooking, a fried chicken supper was well on the way.
The dining room had a long table with a wooden bench on each
side that accommodated five or six each.

Just as the food was about to be placed on the table, in
came a little old lady, the lady of the house. She did not speak
our language and we did not speak hers, so there was no "what
is going on here!" She simply pitched in and helped prepare the

table and put the food on it. Together, we all enjoyed the fellowship and her food. Somebody, and there was about eight of us at the table, passed her a couple of dollar bills, which she accepted and then passed them around the table for each of us to autograph. How gracious! That dear soul had been gone for many years and I often wonder what ever happened to those two dollar bills and how many times she shared with her friends and relatives the details of her experience with those brazen, uninvited American GIs. I have never settled in my mind on exactly what she said each time she told her story. But I have always been able to see the excitement in her eyes and face and hear it in her voice as she told it.

It is strange how when I remember an incident at a time or place, that the memories seem to come in pairs.

A day or so later, as was the practice, our crew was moved to a forward location closer to the battalion company headquarters, as it was our duty to maintain telephone communication between them and our regimental headquarters company. No city limits were involved, but as we passed the last house and topped the hill, the road made a curvy, gradual descent down the hill that leveled into a flat, open field with a small stream flowing through it, somewhat parallel to the base of the hill. The road crossed the stream approximately 200-300 yards from the base of the hill. On the far side of the stream, on the right side of the road, was a small stone stucco building about fifteen feet square. The stone-type roof had been constructed to fit outside the four walls at the top, rather than being placed as a slab on the top edge with an overhang.

This building was about a mile from our company in Fraimbois. With options, that would not have been a first choice for shelter for a forward wire crew operation, but it was the only choice. We set up the switchboard and established telephone communications with our company. Some 155mm howitzers were nearby and seemed to have an abundant supply of shells, and used them. As they let go a salvo, small particles of sand, stone, etc. would fall inside from the edge of the ceiling. For various reasons, when possible, we slept in our sleeping rolls on the floor against the walls. We went back to our company for meals. The top regimental headquarters company officers operated in the company's CP (Command Post), and the company had a full kitchen section.

One morning, after the night had been like all the other nights had been, we went back for breakfast. By the time we had traveled that mile, something had happened. We were told that the line was out from our forward switchboard. So, back we went. The switchboard operator was standing outside and there was no roof on the building. It had fallen inside and flat on the floor and switchboard. Fortunately, it had given the operator just enough warning to let him get outside. No longer than two hours earlier, our crew had been sleeping on that floor.

The Germans had put up stiff resistance all along their side of the creek bank, entrenched under concealment of creek-bank growth. From shrapnel and bullet holes in the German steel helmets, and small bone fragments, particles of flesh and blood inside them and scattered all over the place, many had not left there before losing their lives. Then they were the damn enemy. Now they were nineteen years old, precious sons or husbands of innocent mothers and wives, just like we were.

Story 5

The 314th Regimental Headquarters Company Command Post had been established in a field adjacent to the main highway between Valognes and Cherbourg, Nationale Highway No. 1, approximately three miles south of Cherbourg, on June 24, 1944.

The field was on the east side of the highway at the base of a rather high embankment. By midmorning of June 25, the three battalions were in the process of capturing Fort du Roule and the ring of pillboxes that blocked the descent into Cherbourg. It was deemed necessary to move the CP as close to the battalion CP as possible. The new location was a small field about 500 feet off the east side of the highway on the brink of the plateau overlooking the city. It was a narrow dirt road or lane that reached the field. A small two-story building sat on the city side-corner of the highway and lane. Our jeep parked adjacent to the fence row on the right side of the field, which was lined with trees on all four sides. Unloading my gear, I saw a small hole in the ground that looked like an empty post hole. Realizing that would be the place to start digging a foxhole, I laid claim to that spot by placing my gear right there. Before I had time to do anything else, I heard the switchboard operator tell Sgt. Clarence Glasser of New Castle, Pennsylvania, that the line to battalion was out, but I did not know which battalion. Most likely, it was 1st Battalion.

Sergeant Glasser, a very humble and religious man, had a "I'd like for someone to go with me" look on his face. He could have told some of the wiremen to go. I had only been in the division about four months and had almost no training in telephone communications. I thought to myself, "At least I can go stand guard for him while he repairs the line, once we find the break."

We walked out the lane to the highway and turned right in front of the stone building. At the highway we began the descent down the long steep hill into Cherbourg. The first house was on the left, a short distance from the crest of the hill. We found the break farther down the highway in front of the sixth house. It was a simple break that required no new wire. Glasser had it repaired in short order, and I did not have to shoot at the enemy. We backtracked ourselves, and just as we turned left onto the lane, here came a jeep with Tommy Thompson of Tallahassee, Florida, a switchboard operator, draped over the hood in the same manner a hunter would bring a deer out of the woods. What had happened? Clarence and I had not been on our mission more than fifteen or twenty minutes. The Germans had dropped several rounds of mortar all over the field.

Sgt. George Hersei of Asburn, Pennsylvania, was wounded in the groin. Not knowing what my intentions were for that hole, he had laid claim to that spot and started digging his foxhole when he had gotten hit. Fortunately, it was not a serious wound, and he returned to our company after a few days. Top brass made a quick decision to get out of there and return to our previous PC area.

Some twenty years later, ex-Mstr. Sgt. Carroll Keefer of Baltimore, Maryland, on his way to Orlando, Florida, to visit his brother, stopped in Kingsport, Tennessee, and visited with me. In our long-overdue conversation, he told me what had happened.

A Frenchwoman who enjoyed having the Germans in Cherbourg was in the upstairs of that stone building giving the Germans signals that we had occupied the field. Prearranged plans, I am sure. The Germans seemed to have every inch of France zeroed in, so they lost no time or effort in putting their artillery and mortar fire right on target with the first rounds.

I will never know what happened the woman, but I know what would have happened if news of her had reached us that day! She was captured, but they did not let us know anything about it. The encounter would have been quite different from what she enjoyed with her German comrades. Every day, Tommy Thompson lives in my mind. I visited that general area on a tour in 1993 and progress has changed the area. I could not say for sure, "Right there is that field," even though they have left some of the pillboxes alongside the highway. No amount of progress will ever alter one iota of the whole scenario of that June Sunday morning, 1944.

Story 6

I wish I could give a date and place, but I can't. Certainly France, summer 1944, and probably August.

We were moving forward and it was pitch dark, and the route crossed a large, flat, open field. In fighting a war, one can choose any route he wants to and doesn't have to ask for anyone's permission. In peacetime, this probably had been a large grain field for some farmer. Now it was a shortcut for where we wanted to go.

There had been so much rain in the area, and so many vehicles had preceded us, that the mud almost reached the belly of the jeep. It was necessary for a soldier to walk in one of the ruts holding a "cat eye," a small light with a slit in the middle less than half the size of a stick of chewing gum. It gave a faint glow in the dark. Another soldier did the same in the other rut, each holding the thin flat light behind them as they walked in front of the jeep. This gave the driver some sense of direction and also helped to prevent getting stuck.

A few miles beyond that field, we reached our destination, one of the first houses on the right side of the road in a small rural village, the name of which I will never know. One of our other crews had gotten there earlier that afternoon and had a fire going in the potbelly stove and the room blacked out with thick covering over the windows from inside. As it was late and I had not eaten for several hours, I put a can of C-ration beef stew on top of the stove to perhaps help make it a little more edible.

When it was warm enough, I removed it, and holding it in my left hand against the outside of my right thigh with the tiny can opener, which was like a small hinge with a sharp edge, in my right hand, I punctured the can. Instantly a stream of hot, greasy juice shot upward at a 45-degree angle. Unfortunately, one of us was standing in the wrong place, because about the time that stream reached five feet above the floor, it glazed the left side of Capt. Fred Rogers' face and the rays of the coal oil lamp were at an angle that caused that greasy mess to glisten. After some spontaneous snickers, and not the kind you eat, the silence was awful.

Captain Rogers was the regimental communications officer, and while he would never win a popularity contest, he was a good soldier. All business, his discipline was spelled with capitals. To his back we called him Hawk because his steel, squinty eyes, set in a face of fixed stone, reminded one of that bird of prey. I sure wished I could have eaten those snickers. No one knew what to expect. He finally broke that loud silence with "Campbell, next time, put a hole in the top of that can first!"

My reply was brief. "Yes, sir!"

To this day, I can still see him standing there as straight as a poker, which was always his posture, with the greasy side of his face glistening in the rays of the lamp. I understand that he was from Texas and returned there after the war. He died several years ago.

Next day's daylight revealed that the road had a narrow open field on the right side that extended over to a high ridge, both of which ran parallel to the road as one approached the house. The artillery boys had some 155mm howitzers set up in the field. We had been out working on a line, and as we were in sight of the house, I noticed there was some action around the guns. I also saw a small plane used for artillery observation, flying left to right toward the ridge.

Just as the plane got over the field, a salvo from the guns was in the air. I could not see the shells, but I saw what one of them did at the moment it did it. That little plane exploded and tumbled out of the sky like a robin hit at close range with a .410 gauge shotgun. One of those rounds and that tiny plane had been in the same wrong spot at the same wrong time. How many times would it take before that would happen again, even by everyone trying to do it. How helpless! "His number just came up" could never been more true. I don't believe I will ever witness a more unusual, unbelievable, unreal event.

At the time, fear and other urgent duties and dangers puts such incidents, maybe not out of one's mind, but a way back in it, to one day be released to live with you until your dying day and what you knew about it then is all you will ever know, no matter how much you would like to know about the details. They are lost in a half-century of obscurity.

Carl G. Campbell and Joe W. Campbell (no relation), approximately 1998 (see Carl's story, page 217).

Howard "Benny" Benthine

32nd Infantry Division, 13th Regiment, 61st Battalion, Company C,
Intelligence Division
3rd Division Band

The following article appeared in the Galesburg, Illinois, newspaper concerning my friend Paul Bader and our fifty-year search for each other.

Wartime Experience Leads Man on a 50-Year Search

GALESBURG, ILLINOIS—Two scared kids, far from home, preparing to go to war—little did either know then their friendship would lead a Galesburg man on a search of more than half a century to find his buddy.

Howard "Benny" Benthine, now of Galesburg, but then of Kansas City, and Paul E. Bader, then of Flint, Michigan, were at Camp Fannin in Tyler, Texas, from July to December of 1943 for basic training.

"Our chemistry seemed to click" from the start, Benthine said, and the two 18-year-olds stayed close throughout Infantry Basic Training with Company A, 61st Battalion, 13th Regiment.

Both men agreed it was a sometimes lonely and sometimes frightening time, but both remember some good times, too, including the generosity of Lois and Charles Whitman of Tyler, who befriended many trainees.

"I've been told she was corresponding with as many as 300 servicemen during the war," Bader said in a telephone conversation earlier this week.

Howard Benthine, September 1943.

Eventually, training ended and the young men were separated. Bader was assigned to the 24th Infantry Division. Benthine was in Intelligence, and later in the 32nd Division Band.

Despite an intriguing set of coincidences that included being sent overseas on the same ship and being at the 4th Replacement Depot in Milne Bay, New Guinea, at the same time, they did not see each other again during the war.

After losing track of each other, in fact, it seemed that the friendship forged by the random fortunes of war would remain just a pleasant memory of those dark days. Life went on. Both men married in 1947 and both became fathers twice. Benthine went to work for the Santa Fe Railway, ended up in Galesburg, and retired in 1985, while Bader, a school teacher in Michigan, had retired one year earlier.

That could be the end of the story, but something inside Benthine would not let him forget. Off and on, over more than 50 years, he became somewhat of an amateur sleuth, hoping to find his friend. He knew, courtesy of his correspondence with Lois Whitman, that Bader had made it home from the war, and that he lived somewhere in Michigan.

"I put a tremendous amount of emphasis on friendship, that's just my make-up," Benthine said, trying to explain why he refused to stop looking. "I value friendship deeply."

Fittingly, at the Camp Fannin reunion in April of this year, Benthine ran across a promising lead. Another veteran suggested he write to the editor of the 24th Division News, which he did.

In August, the editor sent a list of five Paul Baders living in Michigan. The third one he called was his long-lost friend. Benthine said he told Bader he had wondered about his whereabouts over the years.

"Paul, I have been looking for you since 1943," Benthine told him.

Bader, although still amazed at the effort Benthine made, also expressed joy that his old friend called him.

"It was a feeling of shock," he admitted, "hearing that voice from the distant past."

"I admire his tenacity," Bader chuckled. "It was pretty tremendous to hear from him."

"I had many times thought about him and wondered what happened to him, but did not know how to contact him," Bader said.

The war years, not surprisingly, were perilous ones for both men. Bader took part in five invasions in the South Pacific, and was in the first wave of three of them.

Benthine won four battle stars in the South Pacific. "Once he went on a 25-man patrol and was the only one out of three patrols who returned unwounded.

"I've said many, many times, 'I wouldn't take a million dollars for having gone through it, but wouldn't go through it again for a million dollars,'" Bader said. Benthine and his wife, Juanita, and Bader and his wife, Larri, met over the Labor Day weekend at the Baders' home in Holt, Michigan. Joining them were Kieth Streeter and his wife, of Durand, Michigan. Streeter had been one of their instructors in 1943.

World War II was one of the defining moments for many men of Benthine and Bader's generation. It perhaps says something about the human spirit that the small, flickering flame of friendship was able to survive long after the fire-storm of that conflict ended.

• • •

My name is A. Howard "Benny" Benthine. I was born April 17, 1925, at Kansas City, Kansas. My parents were loving, devoted, and very thoughtful, but of moderate means during the depression years. When World War II started, I was sixteen and felt surely it would all be over before I reached age eighteen. That was not going to be the case, and on my eighteenth birthday, I, like so many others, registered for the draft. Before the end of April 1943, I received that infamous letter titled, "Greetings, you have been selected by your friends and neighbors to serve our Country." I really didn't think I had been that bad of a neighbor or friend, but I was on my way to learn how to kill and defend our country.

I was inducted into the Army at Fort Leavenworth, Kansas, June 1, 1943. After a lot of instructions I didn't fully understand, and more shots than I can remember, I was loaded onto a train along with many others and headed for a place I had never heard of, Tyler, Texas, and Camp Fannin.

Boy, what a desolate place, and it seemed like miles from anywhere. We detrained and were ordered to line up, get our gear, and marched to a barracks area where we were assigned to a barracks. Each barrack held about thirty men from all over the country. Shortly, we were told to fall out and meet the men who would be training us to kill and to survive, if we were lucky. Basic training lasted seventeen weeks and at times was pure hell!

I became friends with a fellow named Paul Bader, who was from Flint, Michigan, and we stayed together through basic training. During basic, we were at times given weekend passes to go into Tyler, or Kilgore. Kilgore was more open and the men could raise a bit more hell there, however in Tyler, we kept pretty straight-laced. We met a delightful family named Mr. and Mrs. Charles Whiteman, who had a lovely large home on South Broadway. The Whitemans opened their home to the servicemen, giving us a place to relax, visit, and play cards. But on Sunday, we all had to attend the church of our choice. Lois Whiteman kept a record of all the men who had been with them and kept in touch after the war. She was an inspiration to us all.

On Armistice Day 1943, the camp commander thought it would be a patriotic item to have all the men who could, with full field packs, to make a march into Tyler, have a lunch, and then parade around the town square. That is what we did. We had about 20,000 men make the ten-mile march into Tyler and back to Camp Fannin. The citizens could not believe their eyes and some drove along on the return to see if we made it. Many had sore feet and charley horses in their legs, but it was quite a sight to see. I am proud that I made it without any problems. I even went to a dance that evening at the camp.

Following basic, each man was given a delay en route to go home for a few days, as we all were going to another camp. I was placed in charge of twelve other men from the Kansas City area. We all knew when we were to depart and all were on time at the Union Station at Kansas City. We were to take the Union Pacific en route to Fort Ord, California. Having come from a railroad family, I was surprised to see that the Union Pacific conductor would not let us board the train until all the civilian passengers had boarded. To say the least, there were no seats left, so we went into the men's lounge, where there were about four seats, but the conductor would not permit us to be in there. When I asked where we could go, he suggested we stand in the vestibule between the cars.

This was December, and the ground was covered with snow, and as we traveled, the snow would whip up into the vestibules and we nearly froze. At Denver, we had time to eat a hot meal and warm up a bit. When it became time to reboard the train, it was the same situation as at Kansas City. When we arrived in Cheyenne, Wyoming, I told the men to get their gear together, as we were getting off. The station agent greeted us asking if we were going to a near air base. I told him we were going to Fort Ord, California, and that we had been standing since Kansas City, and that we were not going any farther. I told the agent I was calling the air base commander and the authorities at Fort Ord. The agent called for a train master, who said we were to get back on the train. I explained what had happened to us and we were as far as we were going. The train master apparently made some calls and the railroad put an old coach on the rear of the freight train. It had a potbelly stove in each end. We had quite a time finding coal and wood to burn, but at least we were sitting down on cushions instead of the cold vestibule floor. It turned out that several civilians joined us. When the freight train arrived at Green River, Wyoming, we were set on a spur track and told another train would get us later. By this time, several of the men had developed severe colds.

Across from the Green River Station was a bar. I went over and asked for two pints of whiskey. The owner asked my age, and when I told him I was eighteen, he refused to sell it to me. I told him I understood, but to let me tell our story. He ended up giving me the whiskey and food, as we had run out. We had empty food cans, and by melting snow, I was able to fix hot toddies for the men. It sure saved the day, and they did feel somewhat better.

The next day, we were able to get on another passenger train and on to San Francisco. I called the authorities at Fort Ord, advising them of all that had happened to us and that we were already AWOL. In the end, we did make it to Fort Ord and with no other problems.

At Fort Ord, we had about two weeks of additional training. One day we were told that we were leaving for Camp Stoneman at Pittsburg, California, and we would be put on a ferryboat and taken to San Francisco to board a ship for the South Pacific.

Once at Fort Ord, I became friends with a fellow from Philadelphia, Pennsylvania, by the name of Rudy Bernhardt. Rudy was ten years older than me and already married, but had no children. At San Francisco, we boarded a troop ship called the USS *Monticello*, which had been an Italian luxury liner, but that must have been a long time back, as it was in pretty bad condition. We learned there were 10,000 Army troops, plus ship personnel, on board. We also had 132 Navy storekeepers in the hold with us.

As we left the United States, we were permitted to go topside and see our country fade away. For many, it was their last time. There were guards on each level to keep us in our respective holds. We were permitted to be topside for ten minutes in the morning and ten minutes in the afternoon. We ate two times a day at tables about chest high, and the food wasn't fit to slop the hogs with!

We discovered that the storekeepers were eating ship's chow and that it was very good. One day, I asked a Navy fellow about my size if I could use one of his dungarees suits to eat in the ship's mess. I told him if I was caught, I would say I stole his uniform. I went right past the guards and really had a good feed. I kept that up for the rest of the trip.

It took nineteen days for us to reach Milne Bay, New Guinea. When we disembarked, we were told the replacement camp was about ten miles away and that we would have to carry all our gear and walk to the camp. After nineteen days and the poor food that everyone had been eating, this was going to be quite a chore. I ended up carrying both my gear and Rudy's and helping him. As I mentioned, I had been eating much better than most.

About halfway, trucks did arrive and carried us to the 4th Replacement Depot. Apparently, there was a mix-up, as we were temporarily assigned to units in the area. Rudy and I were assigned to the 3752 Trucking Battalion, who were building their campsite in a swamp. Truckload after truckload of rock was brought in. We were to shovel and rake the rock into walk- and driveways.

One day when standing outside the command tent, I overheard the officer in charge telling Sergeant White that they needed more truck drivers. When he came out of the tent, I was leaning on the rake handle. He asked if I had a problem raking, and I said I was a truck driver, not a raker. He called Sergeant White outside and told him to have the motor pool bring over a six-by-six. I thought, what in the hell was I going to go with a board, but I discovered that was an Army description of a certain truck. When the truck arrived, I climbed into the cab and, thank God, there was a gear-shifting diagram on the dash.

Sergeant White and I took off and had gone about five miles when he said to return to the camp. He said that I had passed and asked if there were any others who could drive. I told him that Rudy could but was not as good as me. We both ended up driving, and that officer tried everything he could to have me assigned to him, but we were there to fight as infantrymen and went back to the replacement depot when our orders came in.

We were taken to a liberty ship troop carrier and headed for Finchaven, New Guinea. As we were preparing to get off the ship in Finchaven, someone called out to "catch!" I looked up and there were apples and oranges flying through the air and some ice cream, too. Each man had been issued six rubber bags which would hold about eight to ten of the apples and oranges. Most of us filled our bags. Just as we were about to go over the side, the ship's captain stopped everything until it was determined who had slugged the Navy guard who was guarding their cooler. That was the first I knew about where the fruit had come from. The Army stepped in, and we did get off. We were taken to a makeshift camp area where tents had been put up. We were assigned a tent and had to sleep on the ground.

The next morning, we were told there would be a full layout inspection. A major appeared and entered our tent, as it was the first one in line. We all came to attention and were put at ease. The major asked if anyone wanted to tell him what had happened on the ship. No one spoke up, so I did by saying none of us really knew all the facts, but asked when was the last time he had tasted fresh fruit. He said, "Son, it's been a long time." I said, "Major, it's very obvious we have the fruit, and why don't you help yourself, as I know we can't eat all of it." He took just one bag from each of us and placed them in a duffel bag he had in his jeep. He did the same at all the tents, and that was the last we heard about the fruit.

While at Finchaven, we were introduced to Atabrine, which was to be a retardment for malaria. We were given five pills at one time, and they made me very ill. From that time on, I didn't take too many. All who took them on a daily basis turned yellow, and many did get malaria. I did not get it.

Late one afternoon, we were loaded on a LCT (landing craft truck), to go to Saidor. The LCT had a flat bottom with a flat bow, which was a loading ramp. We were only at sea a short time when a storm developed, and it got very rough. Water was coming over the bow and the deck filled with water where all our duffel bags were. Several men became seasick, and with all that, the deck was one hell of a mess. We had been told to stay out of the two gun turrets, which would be manned by Navy personnel, if attacked.

All of us were soaking wet, and as it got dark, it seemed to get much cooler. I told Rudy I was going to crawl up and get in one of the turrets to get out of the wind. He asked what would we do if we got caught. I said that I didn't think they would put us off. So we did and laid on our life jackets and did get a lot warmer. When we docked, it was daylight, and then we were wondering how to get down without being seen by the Navy.

Well, we got caught and were taken to the ship's captain. He raised hell with us, but that was the end of that. At Saidor, we were taken to a campsite and told to hang our hammocks between the trees and, if the air raid siren sounded, to get on the ground. There was an airstrip and a large fuel depot nearby. We were now assigned to the 32nd Infantry Division, which had already seen a lot of action and had suffered a lot of losses.

That night, sure enough, the air raid sounded. Rudy asked if we had better get on the ground. I said, "No," as the Japs didn't know we had arrived and couldn't be after us that soon. Boy, the bombs and shells were going off all around us and we were afraid to move.

The next morning, Rudy had a large hole in the netting of his hammock, and a large water bag about twenty feet away was in shreds. The next time, we did get on the ground. We were moved by truck about ten miles north to join the 128th Regiment. Rudy was placed with the MPs, since he had been a railroad policeman in civilian life. Since I had studied drafting in school and could read maps, I was put in Regimental S-2, or Intelligence.

The next six months is something I will never forget, as it was the most difficult time of my life. I would go out on patrols with about twenty to twenty-five men per patrol. We would try to work behind the Jap lines and I was to note gun emplacements on maps and check over dead enemy bodies. We never rolled a body until after attaching a long rope, then would get behind something for cover, as they would booby-trap the bodies. I did have a couple blow up on me.

I was to look for any kind of identification as to name, unit, or rank. To say the least, it was a nasty job. After about six months, I was covered with jungle rot from my chest down and had to go to the hospital. The jungle rot was the result of being wet most of the time from sweat, and crossing streams and swamps. At the hospital, the staff would pour bottles of gentian violet all over our bodies, and then we would sit in the sun to dry out.

One evening, the 128th Regimental Band came and played for us, and I really enjoyed the music. The next morning, the doctor advised me that I could not be returned to what I had been doing and asked if I had considered a transfer. This was the first I had heard of their decision. I'm still troubled with the same stuff to this day.

After some thought, I told the doctor that I could play the trombone and would like to get in the Regimental Band. He arranged for me to be auditioned, and I was accepted. The fellows in the band were just great, and I got along with them really good.

I don't remember which month we moved up to Aitape, New Guinea, by a liberty troop carrier. There was no defense of the beach, and we moved right on in. The Navy had shelled the hell out of things. We set up our campsite right along the tree line on the beach. In a couple of days, we learned that a decision had been made to consolidate all division bands which meant the 126th, 127th, 128th, and division bands would be under one command. We ended up with about a 138-piece band, and we played some beautiful music. Our duties varied, from guard duty along the beach, to being ammunition bearers, to loading bombs on Australian planes, and we practiced a lot.

Offshore about two miles, there were three islands. We were told one was a native sacred island, one was PT (patrol boat) base, and we could never get anyone to tell us what the third island was. Then we heard that Bob Hope and his troop were coming to entertain us, and they sure did. He had Jerry

Colonna, Frances Langford, and Patty Thomas with him. I even
got to dance with Patty, and for years, my wife thought that it was
a figment of my imagination. Sure enough, we did see her in a
filmstrip of Bob Hope's travels. When the Hope troop arrived,
we finally learned what was on the third island, as over came a
boat with injured men and a lot of beautiful nurses. They were
the first white women we had seen in ten months.

Our band played the background music for Hope. When
the three bands merged, we had three warrant officers. Two were
sent home, and we retained Eugene Winn as chief warrant officer. He was a great leader and became a good friend.

In October, we were again loaded onto the liberty troop
carrier and taken to Hollandia, New Guinea. We were taken
ashore and to a campsite where we played a lot and entertained
General MacArthur's staff. The landing on Leyte in the
Philippine Islands had taken place just before Thanksgiving,
and the 32nd Division was held at Hollandia in reserve. A couple of days later, we sailed for Leyte, arriving in about a week.
We went ashore and were put on trucks to go to the opposite side
of the island, where we set up campsite on the coral. I don't
know why, but I became very ill with diarrhea and other problems. I ended up losing about thirty pounds.

One night, we got bombed and strafed and were ordered to
dig slit trenches in the coral, which was next to impossible. One
of the men did dig a hole about five feet deep and put a mattress in it. Damn if they didn't send him home as a Section 8.
They put him in a hospital just a few miles from his home. He
wrote back after about a month to one of the men, telling him
everyone thought he was crazy, but now he was home and safe.
Word came down that we were to load up and leave Ormoc for
Tacloban to board ships for the invasion of Luzon.

We were loaded on an LST (landing ship tank) which was
large to hold tanks, trucks, or most anything the Army wanted on
it. The bow (front) was pointed like a normal ship, but it also had
a ramp for loading and unloading. Down each side were quarters
for personnel. Ship's crew was on the stern. Tanks and trucks
were also loaded on the deck. We were in a very large convoy
when we began to get under way. I don't remember just where we
were when we were attacked by aircraft. The sirens sounded, and

that was the signal for all Army personnel to go below deck. I thought if we were hit, it would be mass panic trying to get topside, so I hid under a large truck by the dual set of rear wheels.

Bullets were ricocheting off the deck and Jap planes were on all sides of the convoy. One plane managed to get down between two lines of the ships and I thought, "My God, if they continue to shoot at him, we will all get killed!" I will never know how it happened, but all the ships in the two lines involved stopped firing, but when that Jap plane reached the end of the line, it was all over for him, as the Navy blew him out of the air. Was I scared? You're damn right I was, and I shook for a long time after it was over!

We made the initial landing at Lingayen Gulf on the west side of Luzon. There was a pretty severe firefight, but we all got ashore safely. Also, I was in a position to see General MacArthur come ashore. We moved inland to a town called Tarlac, where we spent the night. The division band was directed to join General MacArthur's headquarters, as we were going to Manila, but would be held at Tarlac until later. We were taken to what had been a country club, and not bad duty. We pulled no duty, just had to play reveille and retreat and practiced a lot.

Right across a large farm field was a rum distillery, which added to our joy. While waiting to get more involved, three of us got permission to be gone for the day. With that, we headed for Manila to see how things were going. It turned out to be a bad decision. We saw firsthand the prisoners who had been held at Santo Tomas University being released after three years. We went downtown along the Pasig River and saw a row of 105mm howitzers firing point-blank into the Walled City. We made it back to Tarlac and were damn glad to be there.

A few days later, we were told to move out for Manila, and darned if we didn't bivouac in the Chase National Bank Building where the three of us had watched the assault on the Walled City. We were then taken to Santo Tomas University to play music for the people who had been freed. It was the first American music they had heard in over three years.

Later, we were taken to Bilibid Prison, where other prisoners had been kept for three years. Most all of these were men from the various military units and were in very sad condition.

Most had made the Bataan Death March. It is something I will never forget. There were dead Jap bodies floating down the Pasig River. We were ordered to get them out of the river, and I was assigned that detail. I had a crew of four, and the first body we tried to get fell apart. I told the men we would go upstream where we had a better access to them, and the mission was completed.

One night we were ordered to go to the apartments along Dewey Boulevard, clean them, and prepare the beds for the top-ranking Army and Navy personnel in the area. Somebody short-sheeted the bed that a Naval admiral was to use, and he, having no sense of humor, made all of us go back about 2:00 A.M. to re-make his bed.

Next, we were told to get all our gear together, as we were going to Malacanang Palace to play the liberation ceremonies when General MacArthur declared the Philippine Islands free of Japanese rule. We did play, and we did get to see MacArthur. We then loaded on trucks and headed back up north to rejoin the 32nd Division. We were headquartered just below Baguio, the summer capital. There were a lot of Japs in the area, and we had to be prepared to fight at all times. After a few weeks and no sign of the Japs, we played a concert before a movie. It was the first to be shown in weeks.

I decided to go back to my tent to write some letters. A new replacement from Michigan decided he, too, needed to write some letters, and we were using a lantern that was in my tent. As we wrote, I heard the sound of an airplane and knew it was "Washing Machine Charlie." I watched him, and he had his wing lights on and finally he went out of sight. Shortly, I heard the sound of wind from his wings. I hit the lantern, turning it off, and grabbed the other fellow, putting him on the ground. About that time, he asked what was happening. The gunfire from the plane started and we heard the sound of bombs going off.

I said, "Let's get the hell out of here!" We grabbed our rifles and headed for the woods. Again, the machine gun fire from the plane started and we hit the dirt, but the plane had turned away from us. When I went down, I ripped my arm open on a tree stump, but at least we were safe. That Jap got a direct hit on ordnance, killing twenty-six men. One of our men, Harry Wilson, went into a culvert, and we had to cut him out of it, as he seemed to be much smaller going in than coming out. We all had a big laugh about it.

After the two atom bombs were dropped on Japan and the Japs surrendered, our division took General Yamaguchi prisoner. Shortly, we were ordered to turn in all our old uniforms and equipment. Since I was now the supply sergeant, I took everything to Manila and drew all new supplies for all the men, including weapons and a new jeep. The reason being, we wanted to make a fresh showing to the Japanese when we entered Japan. We were then ordered back to Lingayen Gulf to board ships and go to Japan.

This was the first part of September 1945, and we were among the first to arrive in Japan. While we were waiting to load at Lingayen, one of the old-time sergeants was accidentally shot in the stomach. He wanted to go with us so badly and was able to convince the authorities he could make it. They permitted him to be loaded. Had we not been in a severe hurricane and had he not become seasick, he might have made it. But he died and we buried him at sea.

The hurricane pitched us around like a bubble, and it was the roughest ride I have ever taken. We landed at Sasebo on the southern island called Kyushu and moved to a town named Fukuoka, on the northwestern part of Kyushu. The band went all over northern Kyushu and southern Honshu, the mail island in Japan.

About December 10, I received orders that I was going home. I, along with several men, went by train to Nagoya and to the 4th Replacement Depot. On December 17, 1945, we sailed for the States on a brand-new troop carrier, and since I was now a staff sergeant, I had some darn nice quarters. We arrived in Puget Sound, December 28 at night, and the sight of all the lights were beautiful. We finally knew we were again safe.

On the 29th, we awoke and went topside, and right alongside us was the Battleship *Missouri*. What a sight that was! We finally got a dock but were told we would have to stay aboard for several days, as the camp was full and there was no room. We were advised that twenty-four hour passes would be issued, dividing the ship down the middle with one side going, then the other. Since I was the ranking noncom for my group, I saw that I had a pass each day and fully enjoyed being in Seattle.

After six days, we were told that we would be moved to Fort Lewis, just outside Seattle. At Fort Lewis, we were issued heavy clothes, fed a great meal, and assigned a barrack, but just as we got into the barrack, we were told to get all our gear, that we were going to get on a train going toward home. It was a long troop train, and we had men on there from various locations in the mid-part of the country. I, along with many other men, was taken to Fort Leavenworth, Kansas. Others went on to their destinations. I was discharged from the Army on January 12, 1946.

I will never forget how wonderful it was to see my mother, father, and sister! We all cried and talked for what seemed like an eternity.

At the beginning of my story, I introduced myself as "Benny." This nickname was given to me at Camp Fannin, and I still carry it to this day.

I mentioned my friend Paul Bader. I knew that Paul made it home and was with the 24th Division, which was near the 32nd Division, all through the war. I kept asking Lois Whitman for his address, but for some reason, she never sent it to me. When we began to attend the Camp Fannin reunions in Tyler, Texas, I kept asking men who had served in the 24th if they knew Paul. One of the men told me how I might find him, and by following through on the lead, I did locate him. It was a heartwarming reunion, and much to our surprise, we discovered that we had gone overseas on the same ship and were at the same replacement depot in New Guinea. Paul has Parkinson's disease and isn't too well, but we keep in touch.

Rudy Bernhardt came back to his wife in Philadelphia. Millie passed away from cancer and Rudy remarried. He also passed away of a heart attack in 1995. We remain friends with his widow, Agnes.

War was hell, and one night we all became men. None who survived will ever forget what we went through for the freedom we all love.

Howard and Juanita Benthine, 1995.

Stanley M. Bockstein, May 15, 1944. Camp Crowder, Neosho, Missouri.
Age twenty-one.

Stanley M. Bockstein

Tech 4-U.S. Army Signal Corps—835 Signal Service BN
Thirty-five months active duty—6-16-1943 to 5-16-1946
CBI Theater 16 Months

The entire following contribution was an address given by Stanley M. Bockstein on April 9, 1995, to those in attendance at the Camp Fannin reunion, Tyler, Texas. Camp Fannin was a camp for basic training, preparing men to enter World War II.

Greetings, fellow World War II veterans and former Camp Fannin trainees. My name is Stanley M. Bockstein of Jefferson, Massachusetts, a suburb of Worcester, Massachusetts, about fifty miles due west of Boston. I'm a retired mechanical engineer.

I, like you, am a Camp Fannin "alumnus," arriving as a private at Fannin on Friday, July 2, 1943, and shipping out as a private first class on Saturday, October 23, 1943, for Denver, Colorado. At this late date, I feel very good about my U.S. Army service, and having communicated my feelings to the CFA Executive Board, the board members graciously gave me this presentation spot on the program.

It is now fifty years since the end of World War II. We veterans wonder, Is anybody out there besides our families and friends going to remember or care about what we did, or where we went during that global conflict?

The United States entered World War II late. The Asiatic part of the war had been raging between Japan and China since

1931. The European part actually had started with German-Italian-Soviet participation in the Spanish Civil War of 1936, followed by Italian conquest of Ethiopia in 1935/1936. All of this exploded into "Blitzkrieg" on September 1, 1939, with Nazi Germany's invasion and conquest of Poland. The Germans had developed a whole lexicon of doublespeak before the war: *Lebensraum*—living space; *Herrenvolk*—master race; *Der Führer*—the leader; *Gestapo* (*Geheime Staatspolizei*)—Secret State Police; *Drang nach Osten*—Drive to the East; *Untermenschen*—sub-humans; *Mein Kampf*—my battle; and so on.

Yes, the United States entered World War II late, but with its vast population of 140 million and enormous industrial strength it was able to put 16 million armed forces personnel and stupendous qualities of military materiel into battle on seven seas and five continents. In just one and a half years, the United States and its allies completely defeated the Axis powers, Germany, Italy, and Japan. Yes, we had good allies—Canada, Great Britain, Australia, the USSR, China—and they fought as well as they could. But they were near defeat at the time the U.S. entered the war after the December 7, 1941, attack on Pearl Harbor, Hawaii.

After the Axis declared war on the U.S. via the Pearl Harbor attack, and Nazi Germany's verbal declaration on December 11, 1941, the United States went to war with a will. Sixteen million young men and women were called up for service, with 12 million max on duty in 1945. Of this, 8.3 million were Army, 3.32 million were Navy, and .47 million were Marine Corps. The U.S. accomplished colossal war-materiel production: 300,000 planes, 634,000 jeeps, 88,400 tanks, 400,000 artillery, 500,000 aircraft engines, 5,600 cargo/merchant ships, 87,000 warships, 6.5 million riffles, 7,600 railway locomotives, and 25 billion rounds of .30-caliber ammunition. Late in the war, the U.S. was putting two ships per day into the water, on the Atlantic, Gulf, and Pacific coasts, and in the Great lakes region.

The Allied political and military leadership, I think, was very good, with the island-hopping campaign in the Asiatic Pacific theater, and the North Africa, Sicily, Italy, rollup of Axis forces, invasion of Normandy, and the drive into central Germany. The U.S. 8th Air Force European bombing was superb, but unfortunately did not include the railway lines to the death camps or selected buildings in these camps, although U.S. bombers flew near these targets on a number of raids.

In retrospect, we wonder what the Japanese military leaders were thinking when they attacked Pearl Harbor. They were a country of 145,000 square miles and 80 million population. In ten years, they had been able to conquer only a small piece of the 3.7 million square miles of China, with a population of about 300 million people. Then they took on the U.S., 4,000 miles away. Actually, both Axis powers were modest-size populations to implement their grandiose, world-conquering schemes.

The Germans did their Axis partner no favors by attacking the Soviet Union, a German ally, in June 1941. The Japanese considered the USSR as its ally also. Then the Japanese did the Germans no favors by attacking the U.S., bringing the U.S. into the war as a joint ally of Britain and the USSR. The ironies of history and of totalitarianism are unfathomable. On December 7, 1941, the Japanese had "strike-north, strike-south" options. If they had struck north, at the USSR, the USSR might have had to surrender in Europe. Instead, they struck south, bringing the U.S. into the war, with the results that we know. Indeed, Admiral Yamamoto told his exultant naval staff after the attack, "I have been to the U.S. Their industrial might is awesome. All we have done is awaken a sleeping giant and filled him with a terrible resolve. We have only one year, after which the U.S. will be unbeatable."

The Nazi Germans also made a few mistakes. First, they did not expect Britain and France to go to war over Poland. They did. They thought the Luftwaffe could dispose of the escaping British army at Dunkirk. It couldn't. They thought the invasion of the Balkans, in April 1941, would not delay their planned summer invasion of the USSR. It did. They intended to reach Moscow in three months. They couldn't. They tried to conquer the Soviet Caucasian Mountains simultaneously with Stalingrad. They couldn't. They thought Operation Citadel at Kursk in July 1943 would destroy the Soviet 5th Guard's tank army. It didn't. They thought Rommel's Afrika Korps would reach Cairo and the Nile. It didn't. They thought the U-boats would win the Battle of the Atlantic. They couldn't. Hitler thought the V-I's and V-2's could win the war for Germany. They couldn't. Reichsmarschall Goering said bombs would never fall on Berlin. They did. Hitler claimed that the Third Reich would last 1,000 years. It didn't. The Germans thought their new encoding "Enigma" machine produced unbreakable decoded radio battlefield messages. It didn't. The Axis powers thought the major democracies couldn't arm and fight a war. They could and did.

So, where do we, Camp Fannin veterans, fit into the worldwide war of fifty years ago? Well, we all answered the U.S. call to arms. We came here to Tyler to the IRTC at Camp Fannin, and left it with an MOS 521 (Infantry Basic). I did mine in the summer of 1943: twenty-mile hikes, infiltration courses, close-order drill, bayonet drill, gas-mask training, rifle marksmanship training, small arms usage, night cross-country maneuvers with maps and compass, and much, much more.

As I and my buddies left for ASTP, Denver, one man said: "That was tough training. I hated it!"

My response was, "Be glad you've got it. It's the best survival training the Army offers. If you get into combat, it will give you a reasonable probability of survival."

Fifteen months later, on boarding a C-57 plane in Miami for overseas flight, we saw crated aircraft engines, tires, and crated medicine, as accompanying cargo. A buddy said, "Stan, we're riding with plain cargo. They don't think much of us." My answer was, " This cargo is high-priority stuff. It's going to get there. If it gets there, we get there." We got there (Calcutta, India).

Have you had much sickness since Army discharge? In the fifty-two years since Fannin, I only had treatment for a hiatal hernia (twenty years ago). I recently found my Army immunization register and counted eighteen inoculations on it between 1943 and 1946. I think all those inoculations gave us some special protection against many communicable diseases, long after the war.

We certainly got used to a variety of food and a variety of lifestyles from sleeping on cots, bunks, bedrolls, and hard floors. We probably could and can sleep almost anywhere. I still remember—"Don't stand if you can sit. Don't sit if you can lie down. Don't stay awake if you can sleep. And, if they offer you food, eat it!"

Armed forces killed were: the U.S. lost 408,000 killed in World War II, Britain lost 398,000 (a large number for a population one-third that of the U.S.), China lost 1.5 million, France lost 245,000, and the USSR lost 13.6 million, twenty-five times the U.S.'s loss, adjusted for population. The Axis powers paid a price: Germany lost 3.5 million, fifteen times the U.S. loss, adjusted. Italy lost 380,000, a rate comparable to Britain's. Japan lost 2.6 million of a 73 million population, about twelve times the U.S. loss, adjusted.

Recently, the media has been carrying articles about the "unnecessary severity" of Allied bombings on Dresden, Germany, and Tokyo, Hiroshima, and Nagasaki, Japan. Well, we veterans have an answer for that. The Axis started the war and has to take whatever consequences ensue. If the Germans have complaints about Dresden, they should tell it to Hitler and Goering. If the Japanese have complaints about the Tokyo fire-bombing or Hiroshima and Nagasaki, they should tell it to Tojo, Hirohito, and Yamamoto.

As for me, I salute the U.S. combat veterans. I was in the U.S. Army Signal Corps and never got into or near combat, while serving sixteen months in the China-Burma-India theater.

I had a good time in the Army. It was the experience of a lifetime, and I'm proud to have served where I was sent. I'll say it loud and clear: God Bless America, the land of the free and the home of the brave!

Thank you for listening.

Stanley M. Bockstein, 1996

Robert Schneier (Marshall).

Robert Schneier

Robert "Bob" Marshall
5th Division (Red Diamonds) 10th Infantry, Company K
General Patton's Army

When I was at Camp Fannin, my name was Robert Schneier. Now they call me Bob Marshall. I came to Camp Fannin, Tyler, Texas, around July 1943 from Fort Devens, as a trainee, and applied for ASTP (Army Specialized Training Program), but did not make it. I was kept on as CADRE (Camp Instructor Acting Corporal), but with no permanent rank. When I saw men I had trained coming out as CPLs, I decided this was not for me and volunteered to go overseas.

I shipped out sometime in August 1944 and went to Scotland on one of the queen's ships. I arrived and was assigned to General Patton's 3rd Army, Fifth Division (Red Diamond), "K" Company, 10th Infantry. I served as a radioman, then company runner.

I was wounded after we took Metz, which was sometime in November, and went over the Autobahn into Germany. I was hit on December 4, 1944. Seriously wounded, having lost my right shoulder blade and a rib, and received a punctured lower lobe, I was hospitalized for some time before being shipped back to the States. I was operated on at the 34th EVAC in Metz, and the group of medical personnel were from General Hospital in Boston, Massachusetts. I was from Brookline, Massachusetts. A couple of days after my surgery, the head nurse came over and

67

looked at me. She looked at my records, then said, "Bobby. Bobby Schneier, don't you know me?"

I had to admit that I did not. It turned out that her name was Capt. Hilda Miller and she took care of my dad in 1935, when he had a kidney removed. She lived in my Zeidi's (grandfather's) apartment for some years and was friendly with my relatives.

She kept me there in the hospital a few extra days, as we were supposed to be out of the evacuation hospital in seven days.

When I did get out, I was taken by train to Paris. After going through rehabilitation for some time, I was flown to England to stay in a place called Cheltenham, a girls' school which had been taken over for medical purposes. While I recuperated, the dentists did some work on my teeth.

Robert Schneier, 2000

From there, I was shipped back to the U.S. by a liberty hospital ship and ended up in Camp Kilmer, New Jersey. My next orders were for Walter Reed Hospital in Washington, where, after being checked over, I was given thirty days' leave and orders to take in plenty of chicken soup and get some rest.

When I returned for the lung surgery, it was deemed that the operation was unnecessary. I left the service with a CDD on May 11, 1945.

Kenneth James

Europe, U. S. Army
70th Infantry Division, 274th Regiment,
1st Battalion, Company E

I was raised on a farm in Arkansas and was drafted into the United States Army in early 1943, at the age of nineteen. I was sent to Camp Robinson, Arkansas, and then to Camp Fannin, Tyler, Texas. I was one of the first to arrive at Camp Fannin for basic training, after which I was held over as Cadre until late 1944, when I joined the 70th Infantry Division at Fort Leonord Wood, Missouri. We immediately shipped out for the city of Marseille, France, where we disembarked and were trucked out to a tent city which was on a hill overlooking Marseille.

Two days later, we loaded on 40 and 8s (unheated trains) and proceeded to Avignon, St. John Rambert, Lyon, Dijon, and Épinal, arriving in Brumach, where we went into combat. Once on the line, we were in combat continually for the next ninety-six days, at which time we were placed in reserve.

On Christmas Day near Brumath, in an old school building, I had just settled down and opened my can of cold C-rations beans, when the entire end of the schoolhouse disintegrated. At that time, my crew and I withdrew to the nearest village, which was about three kilometers back. We received heavy artillery fire for the next several hours. I do not need to tell you, no one got much sleep that night. We then pushed on to Bischwiller, Herrlisheim, and finally, east to Offendorf, on the Rhine River.

Kenneth James, Camp Fannin, 1943.

By January 20, 1945, we were up to Dambach, manning old fortifications of the Maginot Line.

One of our bloodiest battles was at Phillipsburg. One of my buddies was wounded there. At this time, I might add, I had no contact with any of the men from my combat division from war's end until about ten years ago when I joined the 70th Division Association. Then I started corresponding with a few of them, and after several letters were exchanged between James Cummins and me, we realized that I had evacuated him to the aid station when he was wounded. I believe this was near Phillipsburg. He told me later the date was January 9, 1945, my twentieth birthday. Needless to say, my birthday was not celebrated.

Shortly after this, one of our jeep drivers and I were driving along; he had a burp gun and was firing at objects along the road. After another 100 to 200 yards, it fired and the bullet caught him in the right hip, lodging in his knee. At that time, I had to take him to the same aid station where I had taken James for evacuation. The doctor started to examine him and cut the leg of his coverall. He raised hell and told the doctor that those coveralls were stateside starched and ironed, and he had just got them from a new lieutenant who had been killed. When I left, he was still complaining about his coveralls. By the way, James Cummins is a minister in a small town in Indiana today. We have not been able to visit except through letters but are still hoping to be able to meet in person someday.

Anyway, back to the story. We fought on through Forbach in Spicheren Hights, an area overlooking Saarbrücken. My company continued to fight on through Behren, at which time our division headquarters were in Morhange. The winter of 1944 and 1945 was one of the coldest on record in Europe. Our cold-weather casualties were very high.

We were involved in fights in Etzling, Pfaffenberg, Kerbach, Spincheren, Alsting-Zinzing, and the the Kreutzberg Ridge and Spincheren Heights. Then we gained control of the very important Black Forest. During the battle of Forbach and in trying to take Stiring-Wendel, we were on the ridges for thirteen days. We were fighting from foxholes and trenches, and during this time, we lost eleven of our men from sniper fire. We finally realized that the Germans were pulling shifts on us. Every time a German soldier would be killed, he would be clean-shaven and have clean clothes. When we realized what was happening, we ambushed the patrol and liberated Stiring-Wendel, that same day.

Then it was on to Schöneck and the fortification of the German Siegfried line. March 1945, we crossed the Saar River in Saarbrücken. Another buddy, who is now a gynecologist in Syracuse, New York, was wounded by a German mortar shell near the town of Schöneck, France, just five days after his nineteenth birthday. He was evacuated to a military hospital in Dijon, France.

At one point during combat, we had liberated a railroad station in France, and the Germans were trying to take it back. We were fighting in the streets at night, and a bullet creased my steel pot. I guess that was my closest call. On another occasion, a buddy and I had holed up in a French home for the night. Late that afternoon, we were in the front yard, watching our artillery fire on some German gun placement nearby, and watching our bombers flying over head returning to England, after having bombed targets that day.

All of a sudden, we heard a German screaming meemie (a German artillery 88 shell) coming in. We made a run for the front door but didn't make it. The good Lord must have been watching us, because it was a dud. It dug a horseshoe and buried up in the front yard. These were the two closest calls I had during my combat.

The 70th Division had pushed across the Saar River to Saarbrucken with the goal of meeting the United States 3rd Division at Bildstick, Germany.

On March 21, 1945, the 70th Division was taken off active-duty combat and put in the "reserves," after ninety-six consecutive days, having liberated 58 towns, suffered 835 killed (KIA), 2,713 wounded, 397 taken prisoner of war (POW), and 54 missing in action (MIA).

When the war ended, my company was in Wiesbaden, Germany. From there, I was transferred to Bad Hersfeld, Germany, of the 7th Infantry Regiment of the 3rd Division. In October 1945, I enlisted in the Regular Army and continued on active duty until August 1, 1968.

And that's my story, and I'm sticking to it!!!

Dennis P. Spiess

PFC 531st Engineer Shore Regiment

I was twenty-six years old in 1943. On July 15, seven of us GIs were called to report to the top deck of our troop ship in the Mediterranean Sea. When we got there, we were told we were going to invade Sicily and that the seven of us were to go in first. We were teamed up by pairs. Two were to have rolls of white tape to lay out a path in between the sand dunes, so that the first vehicles coming ashore would have an easy time to go inland.

Ed was to have the green, and I to have the red. Before us on the deck was a replica made of sand like the beach we were to land on, with sand dunes and all. We were told to memorize the terrain, so if we landed somewhere else, we could find the area. Ed and I were to place the lanterns on certain high dunes, directing them out to sea so the enemy inland could not see the light. The dunes we were to place them on were several hundred yards apart, and the lights were to tell the powers that be to start the invasion. This would allow the troops landing between them to experience firepower, instead of having the troops for miles along the beach or coastline.

The seven of us were called up to study the coastline replica, three days in a row. The seventh man was a medic.

When time came to board the small landing craft, manned by a coxswain (one who steers a boat) and a Navy lieutenant, the sea was calm and the stars shining bright. We were on our way in twenty to thirty minutes, when a wind came up, very big, dark

Dennis P. Spiess, February 1945, Belgium.

clouds began to cover the sky, and in a short time the sky was still and black. The wind got even stronger and we had to hang on to the sides of the craft to keep from being tossed out.

About this time, the coxswain said to the lieutenant, "I don't know where I'm going, as there are no stars."

The lieutenant replied, "See that star, and that star? Follow them."

The coxswain came back with, "I don't see any."

The lieutenant stated, "Follow them anyhow!

The lieutenant then got his raincoat and pulled it over him. He got his flashlight and his notes of instructions, and after reading them, turned out the flashlight, took the raincoat off his head, and told the coxswain to follow the stars. We all looked up. There were no stars!

At this point, Sonny Vitarelli pulled out his bayonet and said to the coxswain, "Do as the lieutenant tells you or I will jam this up your ass!"

A thought passed through my mind. "We only have seven men aboard and we are going to have a mutiny!"

While this was going on, searchlights from the shore were trying to find us. The waves were so big, they towered over us, at times eighteen to twenty feet. This meant the propeller was spinning out of the water, with the high winds. It could be heard onshore. A searchlight did find us. The Navy battleship far behind us knocked it out, then a third one came on. The Navy also took care of that one.

We finally hit shore. The coxswain dropped the front of the craft for us to get off, and I was the second to last. As I started to do so, a wave lashed me back into the craft. Remember, the sea was wild. Being top-heavy with my backpack, the wave caught me, and as I went down, a machine gun opened fire. The bullets whizzed over, killing the medic behind me. I got off the landing craft in water about knee deep and went up the sand dune. Almost at once, mortar shells started hitting around Ed and I. (You can imagine, no matter how dark it was, when you stood on top of a high sand dune with the sea behind you, you were going to make a silhouette).

I said to Ed, "I'm going up to put up my lantern on this sand dune. Place yours a few dunes over, so we can get some help." Little did we know they were going to call the invasion off, as they thought the GIs would be too seasick to fight. They were going to simply sacrifice us seven, never expecting to see any of us alive.

Six of us did make it. I dug a foxhole on the side of the dune and had barely got in it when a mortar hit close by. The explosion knocked my helmet off and it rolled down the sand dune. I clawed my way out and got it. This took place four times that night, in the same foxhole.

The next thing I knew, it was daylight. GIs were all around me. All I could figure out was that when the fifth mortar hit, it was so close that it knocked me out. During the day, I found out that the landing craft we came in on sank right where it hit shore and was full of bullet holes. If we had needed to evacuate, we couldn't have done so.

Congressman Steve Chabot presents Army veteran Dennis Spiess with a Silver Star for his actions in World War II.

Merle D. Welch

27th Infantry Division, 12th Regiment, Company A
106th Infantry Division
Cpl T/5-864th Engineer Aviation Battalion, Company B
United States Army

I entered the Infantry Replacement Training Center at Camp Fannin, Texas, on January 29, 1945. On May 12, I came home for a twelve-day delay en route, then went to Fort Ord, California. I had thirty days of advanced training, strictly about the Japs and their equipment, then was moved to Fort Lewis, Washington, for a week, and on July 8, boarded the USS *Beaute* for overseas.

We sailed to Eniwetok Island, where we anchored for one week, then formed a forty-eight-ship convoy in which my brother (who was two years older than I) and I were being shipped from Italy to the Philippines to help with the invasion of Japan. We sailed together for a few days, while the first atomic bomb was dropped on Japan. Then, on about the seventh day of August 1945, the convoy split and my half went to Okinawa, landing on August 9. That was the same day they dropped the second atomic bomb, of which we felt the aftershock on Okinawa and thought it was an earthquake.

I had to stay on the boat along with forty-nine others the night of the 9th, to help clean the ship. There were only 1,000 of us GIs on the *Beaute*. They took the other 950 ashore, where they asked for ten or twelve men to go up in the hills and patrol

Merle Welch, 27th Division, Takata, Japan.

to seek out some Japanese possessions. The volunteers had a map and a compass and gathered in an opening to figure out where they had to go. Suddenly, the Jap machine guns opened fire, killing them all.

The other fifty of us got in on the island in the afternoon of the 10th, around 6:00.

They got the whole 990 of us together and told us not to go up in the hills and bunch up, as that was what the Japs wanted, stating that ten of our shipload were already dead. They had loaded us all up on trucks and started away. They drove and drove with us, until it was getting dark. We had been clear across the island and were way back west of an old two-track trail. In the center of the island, on the north side of the trail, was a little field about two acres in size. The trucks stopped and the drivers told us to unload. I got out and asked the driver of our truck what the hell they were unloading us there for. He said that was where we were going and I told him it did not look good to me. He said he couldn't help it, and that was where we were going to be.

All 990 of us got out in that little field. My buddy (Jessie Walcott from Troy, New York) and I went clear back to the far end and lay down on the ground. I was facing the edge, and he and I lay there discussing the situation. All at once, a Jap rifleman with full battle gear stuck his head, shoulders, and rifle out of the bushes and looked me right in the eyes. He looked over the whole field of us and then left. I said to my buddy, "There is a goddamn Jap," and he said, "Where?" I said, "Over there. He just stuck his head out of the bushes!" My buddy said, "Let's get him!"

The only weapons any of us had were hunting knives that were sharp enough to shave the hair off your arms. We took off after him and chased him for about 100 yards. I stopped Jessie and told him we better get back to the field before we get our asses shot off. We went back to the field and I told him that what we have to do is go all over the field and tell everyone that there are Japs around and for them not to go to sleep. We decided that half of us would have to stay awake while the other half slept. Jessie and I divided them in half and we each went and told them what was going on.

All they did was laugh at us, thinking we were just joking. We told them not to laugh, as it was not funny. Jessie and I were only Pfcs, but due to me seeing the Jap, I felt it was my place to take command of the bunch, so I did. We would each keep checking on them during the night to make sure that around one-half were awake.

Everything went good, in the meantime. There were small firearms back and forth over our heads, and come to find out, the two-track trail that we were on ran down through the valley. The GIs that were on mop-up duty were on the ridge to the south of us and the Japs were on the ridge to the north. We were on the Japs' side of the road, with no weapons to defend ourselves. Just at daylight the next day, a jeep with a driver and a colonel came pulling up from the east.

They stopped and the colonel got out. I ran out to where he was. He asked, "What the hell are you guys doing here?"

I told him, "This is where they dumped us out last night, sir."

He told us, "Get the hell out of here. You're right on the front lines! Hit the road, in double time!"

After we had run a few miles, we came upon an engineer outfit. The colonel stopped us there and asked at their kitchen if they had anything to feed about 1,000 hungry men. Their eyes stuck right out of their heads.They were only used to feeding small groups of men. They cooked up some pancakes and each man got half a canteen of coffee.

When we were done eating, the colonel said they had been looking for us all night. They could not figure out what had happened to us. We hit the road again and headed south for a few miles. Thanks to all the walking and double-timing at Camp Fannin, Texas, we were prepared for it when it came time for battle. We finally came to a field where they were to have taken us the night before, and there was a lot of brass there. They split us up for replacements for all the outfits on the mop-up. They figured there was somewhere around twelve to fifteen thousand more Japs to be killed off.

I was put in Company A (battalion unknown), the 12th Regiment of the 27th Division and the 106th Infantry. Company A was in the rear for rest and recuperation for two weeks, building back up their strength to go back up on the line. I replaced a Mexican boy who had just won the Congressional Medal of Honor for knocking out two Jap pillboxes single-handedly with a BAR that had Company A pinned down. Everyone wondered why he risked his life to do what he did. He appeared to be in a daze.

On the morning of August 14, we had to go up and start killing Japs. The company commander got up before us and said that the Japs had just surrendered. Just before the commander told us that, I had wondered to myself and said, "Lord, what am I doing here? I could be back home on our 300-acre farm if I had not volunteered to do my part over here."

We started getting ready to go into Japan for disarmament and occupation. We were given two boxes of brown shoe polish. One box was for each of our combat boots so that we would look good going into Japan. We all polished our boots.

On August 28, 1945, we boarded C-54 planes after bivouac on the airfields for two days and nights, in the rain and mud. Our combat boots sure did look good, though. We then got off Okinawa around 9:30 in the evening and landed in Japan around 1:30 the next morning. We arrived at Osaka, a field that the Americans had terrific directions to, but there was no one to tell us where to go or what we were to do.

Someone said that there was an airplane over there in the hangar. We walked over and saw a pile of plywood they had stacked, so we spread it out on the floor. At this place, again, I would not let my buddy go to sleep. I made it so that one of us had to stay on guard. We would change guards about every four hours. About daylight, our company found us and got us out to some old Jap barracks where we stayed for a short time, then started disarmament. We disarmed the beach that we were supposed to have hit when the invasion took place November 1, 1945. Thank God we did not have to go through that, as I don't think the first wave or two would have made it—it was fortified to the butt. We spent four months in disarmament; the last place we disarmed was over the west side of Japan at Takata.

Finishing up there just after Christmas 1945, the 27th Division, from New York State, broke up and came home. Those of us that did not have enough time in the Army to get out were sent to other outfits. I was sent to the 860 Engineer, just outside

Yokohama, and spent one month there before being taught to operate bulldozers and to spread gravel at the 4th replacement depot. After that, they called for more men and operators up forty miles north of Tokyo at Yokota airfield. There I was put into Company B of the 864th Engineer Aviation Battalion, as an operator. This was my assignment until the Army needed mechanics for heavy equipment, which is where I stayed until leaving Japan on September 9, 1946, aboard the USS *Hood Victory*.

When I was with the 27th Division, I spent about two months doing carpentry work. I fixed the barracks building and toilet seats for the latrine, and built boxes for the guys to send their souvenirs home, such as rifles and swords that they had taken away from the Japanese (those dirty rats!!!).

I think all of us GIs that went over to Okinawa on the USS *Beaute* should have been given combat infantry badges and a battle star for what we had to endure. We never got anything, as we were not assigned to an outfit yet. I personally should have been given a medal of some kind for having taken command of 990 men throughout the night.

I did, however, receive the Asiatic Pacific Theater Ribbon, the Victory Medal, the Good Conduct Medal, and the Army of Occupation Medal Japan.

I was "all I could be"!!

Merle Welch, 2001

Vito Ludovico

The 11th Medical Supply Depot-U. S. Army
National Guard

My military experience all began in December 1942, when I was inducted at Fort Devens, Maine. The weather was very cold. After receiving uniforms and equipment, we boarded a troop train, not knowing where we were going. We hoped we were going south, preferably to Texas, where the weather was warm. Sure enough, we went to Fort Sam Houston, San Antonio, Texas, to a subsidiary of Fort Sam called Dodd Field, which was built to accommodate all the soldiers.

Dodd Field was a tent city with four men to a tent. I had basic training there, and afterward, our outfit became "The 11th Medical Supply Depot." We were considered limited service because our outfit was made up of men with physical disabilities, like a crooked arm, an eye missing, etc. I had a very bad ankle and still do. Our outfit was not suited for the rigors of the infantry.

The Battle of the Bulge came, and many in my outfit passed a more liberal physical exam and were shipped overseas to join the war. I flunked again. It was hard to get a promotion to PFC. Some of us became acting squad leaders or acting platoon leaders, but no stripes or money went with the job.

One day a notice was on the bulletin board about an opportunity to attend lab, x-ray, surgical, and pharmacy technician school. I signed up for the lab course, and we all received cor-

Vito Ludovico, Dodd City, San Antonio, Texas, Tent 1.

poral stripes on starting the various courses. In three months, we graduated. That ended my tenure at Fort Sam Houston, and I was shipped to Camp Fannin, Texas, which was just starting to open in 1943. I was assigned to the station hospital and to the laboratory department. My barracks was right on the road between the hospital and the still-existing smokestack. The barracks was also home to the hospital personnel, lab, x-ray, surgical, and ward boys. I don't remember how many barracks it took to house all the hospital personnel, probably three. I met my future wife at the First Baptist Church Service Center. Her Sunday school class were sponsors that night, providing refreshments and games for the soldiers who attended. We went steady until we were married on March 9, 1946.

One of the duties of our lab was to help the pathologist who was in charge of our lab in performing autopsies on soldiers killed in training accidents or who died for whatever reasons. The morgue was situated real close to the smokestack, probably ten to thirty yards away.

My fiancee's uncle had a watermelon patch about twelve miles out on the old Dallas highway. One day he asked me to come out to his patch and get some watermelons. I got a couple of guys, went to the patch, and brought back about twelve watermelons. It was summer and real hot, so, in order to keep the melons cold, we put them in the body trays in the morgue.

In our lab, we used a chemical they called Methylene Blue, which was used to run tests. But we also used it to play tricks on our fellow hospital staff members. We would slip a few drops in their coffee or tea and listen for screams when they passed their water (urinated), because it would be turned dark blue.

The month of March is a very significant month to my family, because my wife's mother died on March 6, 1990, I was discharged from the Army on March 7, 1946, March 8 is my wife's birthday, and we were married on March 9, 1946.

My military career consisted of three and a half years in the Army and about thirteen years in the National Guard.

This verse was printed in the *Guymon Daily Herald Pioneer Edition*, April 13–14, 1985. It is reprinted here by permission of the No Man's Land Museum in Guymon. It is a fitting end to the chapter, reflecting as it does fifty years later some of the sentiments of those who were witnesses to the rabbit drive.

The Rabbit Drive
By Jennie Mouser

We lived in the Dust Bowl and Depression days,
And the weather had its part to play.
We tried to raise some feed and grain.
To keep our animals alive was our big main.

It was so dry and the rabbits were thick.
To get rid of them we needed a trick.
They ate a lot of our feed and grain,
So to have a rabbit drive was our gain.

We went to the sand hills for the big drive,
Which took place, April fourteenth, nineteen thirty-five.
It was an unusual calm and beautiful day.
And a big crowd gathered from miles away.
The excitement was all around.
To get the rabbits, they all were bound!

They had made a huge wire pen
To drive all the rabbits in.
There were hundreds of rabbits in that drive,
And none of them were to stay alive.

They should have sensed the warning that day.
As the black storm cloud was headed their way.
But all that mattered and filled their minds
Was the number of rabbits they'd get this time.

When they got the rabbits to the edge of the pen,
The storm hit fast and the screaming began.
It was so black, blacker than any night.
My, it was a horrible sight!

It folded over us like a wave.

The dust was so thick we couldn't breathe,
And we wondered what to us it would lead.
We began to think this might be the end,
And we had no time to make amends.

They threw down their clubs and sticks and stones.
It seemed as if each one was all alone
Women and children were crying and praying then
That they could just be with their families again.

Then the wind started to blow,
And some of the dark clouds started to go,
And a little daylight we began to see
So everyone could get where they needed to be.

Now I never did mind to see a rabbit shot,
As I always thought it was part of their lot.
But I thought they should be given a chance some way
For some of them to get away.

And now I would like to have my say
About the rabbit drive that day.
I think an Upper Hand was waved
And all those rabbits' lives were saved!

Vito Ludovico, 1985

Elmer T. Horne, Jr.

ETO 13th Armored Division, 15th Regiment
63rd Battalion, Company D
58th Quartermaster Corps
Calvary Reconnaissance Squadron

I was born on January 14, 1925 in Thomas County, Georgia. After high school, I went to military school at Gordon Military College in Barnesville, Georgia. Shortly before graduation, in the spring of 1943, the Department of Defense held an examination for seniors all over the U.S. The Army called the program the Army Specialized Training Program, ASTP for short. After graduation, I was inducted into the service and stationed at Fort McPherson, Georgia, where I was advised that I had qualified for the program and asked if I wanted to enter. Theoretically, what we were supposed to do was to be sent to college after basic training and stay there until we received certain training and then be commissioned right off. At eighteen years old, this was a big deal. But in February 1944, the program was disbanded.

In the meantime, on August 16, 1943, I was transferred to Camp Fannin, Texas—one more hellhole—to complete the basic training. Fannin was a major Infantry Replacement Training Center, and eventually a quarter of a million men trained there. The camp only stayed in existence from 1943 until 1946.

Before the ASTP disbanded, our one little tiny group, which amounted to about 2 percent of the total people that ever

Pfc. Elmer T. Horne, 1945.

Mr. and Mrs. Elmer T. Horne, Jr., 1995

trained at Fannin, were all put together in one battalion because we were going to college. We were trained by Army guys who hated our guts because we were "schoolgirls." They also called us "ball-bearing WACS" and all that stuff, and treated us pretty rough. There weren't any restrictions on what they could do to us.

General McNair, who was head of the Army Ground Forces, did not like the Army Specialized Program, so many interviews and tests were given to the trainees throughout the time at Fannin, and many fell by the wayside. But I made it and eventually was shipped off to Louisiana State University in November 1943. From there I was sent to Camp Lee, Virginia, to the Quartermaster Corps, noncombatant, where the 58th Quartermaster Base Depot was shipped overseas, landing in England. A quartermaster is an Army officer who provides clothing and substance for a body of troops.

In early 1944, we were in Liège, Belgium, where the Battle of the Bulge busted out. Liège was one of the targets because we were one of the biggest suppliers of rations, clothing, etc., in the continent. The Germans planned to wipe us out, and they were dropping buzz bombs. They dropped a lot of them on Antwerp. Liège was between where the Germans were and Antwerp. We were in Liège because we had these vast acres of gasoline dumps and ammunition, so we were good targets. It was hit or miss for us during the Bulge, and there were a lot of causalities for us.

I was in a cavalry reconnaissance squadron, which is about the equivalent of scouts for the Army. We moved about mainly in jeeps or something called armored cars. We also had some light tanks, and were part of the 13th Armored Division. I got very limited combat. Most of the armor in an armored division is not in cavalry reconnaissance—it's in the tank battalions and the armored infantry.

By now, we were moving down in southern Germany. I was assigned to be the machine gunner of a .50-caliber machine gun mounted on a tripod back between the seats of a jeep. As we drove along the road, headlights suddenly were coming our way. The lights turned into columns, then went out. When we got to where it seemed that the lights had gone out, we could see that it was a farmhouse. We stopped, and I got out and thought I'd go find some Germans.

All of a sudden, I was standing right in the middle of a bunch of them, Germans, I mean. I turned around a corner, and talk about being scared! But they were more scared than I was, because up the road there we had this whole armored task force. They heard 'em coming. When they were coming, we were "Vroom, vroom, vroom" coming down the road with our big guns. And they were a rear-echelon unit anyway. They weren't combat, and they were scared to death even though there was nobody but me.

In the jeep, I had my .50-caliber machine gun, but had a pistol on my hip. I threw it up the air and started shooting away and then took my rifle butt and broke out a few windowpanes. By this time, they weren't giving any resistance at all. They surrendered, about eight or ten, one of them a woman. I motioned for them to go that way, back there to the MPs and the prisoner-of-war enclosures. By now we were capturing so many Germans that it was no big deal. But it was a big deal for one person to capture eight or ten by himself!

When I got out of the quartermaster corps, I was sent to a combat outfit, the 13th Armored Division, one of two divisions designated to make the assault on Japan. The Army then decided they were going to make an amphibious assault on Japan, which required a different kind of tank. They told us to go home. We left Europe right away and were sent home for our thirty-day rehabilitation. Then the A-bomb was dropped.

We reassembled at Camp Cook, California, where we were supposed to have taken our preinvasion training. We'd beaten the odds in Europe and we were all alive. When we pulled into Boston Harbor, the boats all came out to meet us. The war was over, and they came out with the banners.

I received a Combat Infantry Badge, a European Theater of Operations Ribbon with three battle stars, a Victory Medal, a World War II medal, and a medal of Good Conduct. I also got a medal for serving in the Korean War.

Lawrence G. (Jack) Lovett, 1940s.

Lawrence G. Lovett, 2000

Lawrence G. Lovett

Staff Sergeant, Infantry
13th Regiment, 61st Battalion, Company A
Combat Cadre

I was inducted into the service on July 21, 1944, in Houston, Texas. I entered Camp Fannin, Texas, with papers showing that I had blue eyes, brown hair, was 5'6", weighed 134 pounds, and had two dependents. My Army career was very short, only about eighteen months. Three times I signed up and passed the test for paratroopers, Fort Benning, Georgia, having the orders cut and sent to Camp Fannin, and all three times Camp Fannin rejected them, saying they needed me worse than Fort Benning did. I trained the infantrymen to shoot. My classification was rifleman instructor–expert infantryman.

Camp Fannin was an infantry training replacement center. Upon completing a hard seventeen-week training, the men had a ten-day furlough, then were sent straight overseas to fill in the gaps left by the men who had been killed in action. The field commander wrote to Camp Fannin stating that he did not want the troops to be sent to fight until they had a furlough, as they were being trained so hard that they would give out before they got to the front.

I had no major problems with my physical or mental well-being except for my left arm. During bayonet practice, I went through one of the targets all the way and messed up my left elbow. I got three days' light duty, which meant that I didn't have to carry my rifle for three days. During this time, I remained with my unit but was given the duty of stack guard, which meant that I was to stand at parade rest at the head of a group of rifles that had been stacked, waiting for them to take their training and exercise as log rollers. While this was taking place, a lieutenant whom I had never seen before and have never seen since came down the field behind me. He wanted me to give the names of all the people behind me from my platoon, all the way to the president of the United States, which took quite some time. And with a ten-pound rifle being held up at a rifle salute, I was really about to give out by that time, because my arm was about to fall off. My right arm was holding the rifle the whole time. I had told him prior to him making me follow his command that I had been given light duty for three days, because of an injury to my elbow, so he was aware of the fact that I had been hurt.

I told the first sergeant of my platoon when I went in that evening. He quizzed me on what the fellow looked like, so I gave him as close of a description as I could remember. He said, "I'm gonna see that that sucker goes overseas and gets out of our camp." I never did hear any more, until about ten days to two weeks later, I heard that he had found the man and he had been sent to France. Hearsay related to me that he was shot in the back on his third day of battle. I never heard any more about him, only that he was a second lieutenant right out of school, sent to Camp Fannin.

During part of my stay at Fannin, I was able to be a company commander, and on a Sunday afternoon, I formed our company and with acting "gadgets," who are just people you pick out of your platoon to put in charge of your squads, I took our company to the post and reported it to the general. The whole camp was reporting to the post. I was scared to death the whole time, but I enjoyed doing it. I had never done it or seen it done.

My first duty with the troops after I had finished my training was when I was put into A-61. There I stayed for the rest of my career at Fannin. I was to walk my troops around in the quadrangle, teaching them how to march, obey commands, etc., and as a rookie who had never given a command in my life, was again scared. One guy spoke out right in the middle of the ranks and told me, "Sergeant, you gave that turn on the wrong foot."

Well, I wasn't a sergeant to start with. I was a buck private. So I halted the group and told him, "I don't want you to ever open your mouth to me again, in rank. That is breaking every rule in history, to speak when your commander is in charge. Now, you get back in rank, or before this is over, you're gonna be washing commodes for the next two weeks." He apologized and went back in line and I didn't have any more trouble. Incidentally, he was a colonel in the ROTC. But I told him, "We're not playing Boy Scouts here, We're playing Real McCoy," which kinda degraded him, too, somewhat, I guess.

Another time I remember so vividly concerns a boy about 6'2", weighing about 190 pounds. We were throwing live hand grenades and were in a foxhole with a firing shelf on it. We stepped up on the firing shelf to throw the grenade. I talked him through the procedure by telling him to put the grenade behind his ear and throw it like a football, when I counted to three. When I got to three, he turned it loose and it rolled down his back and hit the bottom of the foxhole, and we had five seconds before the thing was going to explode. So I grabbed it and threw it out of the pit. It got up about fifteen feet into the air before it exploded. No one was hurt.

My buddy, who was a platoon sergeant, and I did all the teaching of dynamite, TNT, booby traps, and all the ordnance to be done in the field. We had a problem going, whereas a machine gun problem was set up down the bayou in front of me, which was supposed to look like a machine gun. I had caps pasted all the way down the thing about six feet apart, and they went off of a trickle board. You would just drag a wire down a series of posts, and it looked like every time it hit one of the posts, it would fire. It looked like a machine gun shooting.

On this day, we were having an inspection by a a full colonel from Birmingham, looking the situation over. When he saw that ordnance go off down in that bayou out in the water, he stopped the program because he thought it was live ammunition. After I explained to him what it was, he resumed with the program. After he was finished, he didn't leave, but hung around watching everything, just getting in my way. So I had a quarter-pound of TNT in the water out in front of us, about five or six feet from the bank. He kept walking around with his little trainee stick under his arm. He walked down close to the water, and I guess the devil got hold of me. I fired that TNT, and it "rained" for twenty minutes seemed like. I wet him from one end to the other. He jumped into his jeep and left, and I never saw him again!

Another time, I had been giving behind-the-line instructions out at the rifle range. I had about 100 rifles up on the range shootin' all the time, and with all of them firing, you couldn't hear it thunder. I was out there teaching a class of about seventy-five kids spread behind the lines, waiting for their turn to go up and shoot. I was told that we were going to be inspected that day by Birmingham again. They sent a general out to look our situation over, in a jeep with a driver and all. Prior to him arriving, I told my boys that I had lost my voice and could not talk, but could holler. I said, "So I'm gonna get up there and beat the tar out of that bunch of papers hanging on the rack, and act like you're really getting a lot of good instruction when that jeep comes up. Now I want four of you to go in different directions, and the first one to see the jeep, come charging in here and everybody get off, and get up and be sittin' there looking at the chart and paying attention to what I'm saying, and put out your cigarettes."

Sure enough, the general drove right up to where I was giving instructions, sat there for three or four minutes, then drove away. I got a commendation for giving the best behind-the-line instructions that he had inspected on his trip.

At Camp Fannin we did bivouac training with live ammunition. One day I heard a sound that was different. I said to the lieutenant, "That's a short round, We better hit the ground!"

He said, "Naw, it's not."

"Yes it is," I yelled, and I hit the ground with him right behind me. It was a good thing, because a piece of that ordnance about a foot long went right between us. We were about thirty feet apart. It plowed that field, right between us. It had been raining for two or three weeks, and some of the powder charges didn't go off, so that made it come in short on us.

I had another buddy, Sgt. Bill Erwin. Just as they gave the signal for the men to go, one of his men started firing. Bill was standing about fifty yards in front of us with his legs apart, had bent over to do something, and the soldier was shooting between his legs, eight rounds. On the eighth round, I picked up a tree limb and knocked him loose from his gun, and took it until he could settle him down. That's typical of young men who have never had live ammunition in their hands. He had no idea that he was putting anyone in danger.

In another incident, I was firing a machine gun on one of the problems, and they were supposed to come up to this place, fire into the machine gun nest, and put me out of action. We had full-sized targets of a man. They were supposed to shoot at it, then buoyant it as they went through. The soldier evidently liked my profile better than he did the target. He hit me on my left arm, just outside the bone area. He backed up and hit me again with it, in the same place. I was glad he wasn't a very good buoyant man, or he would have hit me right in the heart. Then he went right on over the hill with the rest of the troops.

When we were given a charge of dynamite, if we discovered that it had crystallized, it couldn't be turned back in to supply, but we had to blow the charge. But one of the fellows went to turn some in to the depot and dropped a stick. It hit right beside of his foot, blowing the whole back end of his foot off, from his ankle down, and blew his shoe all to pieces. That was the only casualty I know of in the whole time I served at Fannin.

My discharge from Company A-61 Training at Camp Fannin was on December 21, 1945. My discharge papers showed that I had earned decorations and citations from American Theater Campaign Medal, Good Conduct Medal, and World War II Medal.

• • •

Author's note. Mr. Lovett's story was sent to me on tape. Several times during his recording, he said that he was not a "hero." Every man and woman who served at any capacity in World War II was and always will be "a hero." Had it not been for the effort of all service personnel and those who kept the home fronts going while they were away, our world would surely be a different place today.

We own a debt of thanks to the entire generation—men and women who worked in the factories to supply the servicemen and women on the front with needed ammunition and supplies, those who worked on farms to keep the nation from going hungry, those who cared for the families while others were away—yes, the entire generation pulled together for the good of our country. You are all heroes.

Tommy B. Slaughter, 1940s.

Tommy B. Slaughter

77th Division, 305th Infantry Regiment,
82nd Battalion Company B
Pioneer in the II and III Battalion Headquarters Companies
Pacific Theater—Philippines and Okinawa

I was assigned to a rifle company in Camp Fannin, Texas. After three days, I was reassigned to a specialized training battalion where I received the same basic training as the rifle company. There I graduated from Army Intelligence and Reconnaissance School.

The last thing the teacher told us was, "Uncle Sam has spent $10,000 on each of you for this schooling. Now don't go out there and get your ass shot off!" I had his warning in mind several weeks before he even mentioned it.

I served as a pioneer in the II and III Battalion Headquarters Companies, 305th Infantry Regiment, 77th Army Division, in the Pacific theater. Each battalion headquarters company had a squad of pioneers consisting of twelve soldiers, one sergeant, one corporal, and ten privates and/or privates first class. The word *pioneer* means a small body, such as a squad of foot soldiers in advance of the main body. In World War I, this was known as No Man's Island.

The Jap soldiers would locate a cliff, a third, a half, or three-fourths of the way up the hillside. They would dig an opening about two feet square into the cliff. After entering the cliff two feet, they would dig a room probably ten feet square.

They would use the cave as a fortress, shooting American soldiers who were trying to take the hill.

Duties of the pioneers were to make flame-fuel, to travel back and forth by foot during battle delivering flame-thrower fuel and all necessary ammunition up to the rifle companies on the front lines. Pioneers had the hazardous duty of blowing up the caves.

Beach Head

We were making a beach landing, rifles were firing, machine guns blasting, mortars dropping and exploding, and artillery dropping in. I decided rather quickly that a person could get killed. The sailor had dropped me off and left me. I decided that I could not swim across the ocean. The enemy seemed to be awfully mad, and I didn't do anything to make them that way. Without hesitation, I got in a hole for protection. We were taught in basic training not to enter a Jap cave.

I knew I needed lots of protection and quick! Not knowing what to expect, I jumped in a Jap bunker. To my surprise, there were five Japs inside. Their heads, arms, and legs were scattered all over the bunker, blood was everywhere, and they were all dead.

The Dud Removal Detail

A dud is a shell that fails to explode after being fired. Our bivouac area had a few duds lying around it. A person in the military learns very quickly that there are three ways to eradicate the problem: the right way, the wrong way, and the military's way. Anyone but the military would have solved the dud problem the safe and correct way by moving the bivouac area and leaving the duds for the enemy to deal with. After all, they put them there.

The four of us, and the officer who had a shovel in his hand, were standing around the duds. We were being instructed to pick them up, carry them out of the bivouac area, and bury them. Any movement of the dud could have caused it to explode. We handled those duds gentler than any female ever handled her offspring.

Perimeter Defense

If at all possible, our headquarters company would establish a perimeter defense just prior to night. This was a circle of foxholes approximately 100 to 200 feet in diameter. The fox holes were about 10 feet apart. The Jap civilians were warned not to move about at night. We shot everything that moved around at night, even our own men. We didn't take any chances.

We were in our foxholes for the last time before the final battle the next day. About an hour after dark, a soldier on the opposite side of the perimeter from me shot and killed a woman who had a baby strapped to her back. Evidently, the baby was not hurt. The child cried for about thirty minutes. I heard a soldier holler out, "I can't stand to hear that poor baby cry! Throw up a flare. I'm going to crawl out and get that baby."

After he got it, the baby stopped crying. I will never know if it was a boy or girl or if it is still living. He or she would be about fifty-five years old by now.

The next morning, we, the III Battalion, moved through the I Battalion, who were in possession of Hill 79. Our objective was Hill 85. We had just returned from delivering a case of grenades to the front line. Orders came back that a rifle company was pinned down halfway up Hill 85, by Japs in the cave.

"Archibald and Slaughter—ordered to blow the cave!" came the orders.

We each carried a fifteen-pound satchel charge of TNT to the opening in the cave, pulled the pin, and tossed it in. We had to run as fast as possible to get out from under the falling debris. Archie was wounded slightly from falling fragments. Thank God for the two expert riflemen who kept us covered when we were executing our hazardous duties.

Mined Road

We were bivouacked on a mined dirt road, in Tank Valley, west of the main road from Shuritown, to the town of Naha, Okinawa. Each day we had to walk the half-mile of mined road to the main road to pick up water and food supplies.

Tommy Slaughter, 1999

Three soldiers walking the mined road, behind Stanley Halicka and I, stepped on a mine. It killed and blew off the leg of the man who stepped on it, and wounded the other two badly. When my buddy and I went back, I noticed my tracks were within two feet of the mine.

W'hayland Greene

Staff Sergeant
3rd. Squad, First Platoon of Company "C," 1st Battalion,
126th Infantry
Division of the 32nd Division

Greene entered the Army in August 1943 at the age of eighteen, in Vivian, Louisiana. He was shipped to Camp Beauregard, Alexandria, Louisiana, for two weeks' training in the areas of following orders, KP, and how to carry out guard duty. KP means "Key Point," which is the location or installation which is of strategic importance such as docks, government or administrative buildings, power installation, etc. He was then transferred to Camp Fannin, Texas, for seventeen weeks of basic training, in preparation to be sent overseas as infantry replacements for men being sent back who had been wounded or killed. After basic training was completed, he was sent home for ten days before leaving for California, with New Guinea his destination, followed by the Philippines.

The Philippines proved to be Greene's first experience with death, that of seeing both American and Japanese soldiers killed. The first Jap he killed haunted his mind for almost two weeks. Every time he closed his eyes, whether it was day or night, he could see the man he had shot, totally in a "kill or be killed" situation.

The battle at Leyte lasted for forty-seven days. It rained all forty-seven days, which meant the men slept in foxholes filled with three or four inches of water, sleeping only one or two

103

S. Sgt. Whayland Greene, age twenty, 1945.

hours at a time. They were often cut off from the ration supply line, which meant going for days without food. Waking up to a can of cold C-rations, such as cold spaghetti or meat, and having to fight the flies that had just flown from the bloated bodies of dead Japanese, was a revolting thought, but when a soldier had gone for days without food or water, he'd eat anything.

"Can you picture wrapping one of your buddies (who was killed near you) in a poncho, burying him, then going back after the battle was over, digging him up, putting him on a litter, and carrying him for miles on a narrow jungle trail? The odor was almost unbearable. When you see these war pictures, you never smell the horrible odor. Be thankful you don't! It's an experience that will never be forgotten. I never go to sleep without giving thanks for food, water, and shelter," Greene says.

At one point, Greene and a buddy were sent out to see what was ahead. When they saw some enemy soldiers, the lieutenant told them to turn around and come back. As they were running back, the Japanese opened fire with a machine gun and hit his buddy in the back of the head, killing him instantly.

Upon arriving back at the camp, Green's feet, which were badly infected with jungle rot, were really hurting. The men had suffered from twenty-six days of being wet, as it had rained night and day throughout this time. When the lieutenant saw Greene's feet, he immediately sent him to the field hospital. His boots were almost rotted off, and the doctor had to cut his socks off, because they had grown to the skin. Blood came off with the rotten socks. After having been wet for so long and spending a lot of time in the mud, the canvas cots felt like a luxury hotel.

By the time the battle on Leyte, Philippines, was over, the forty-seven-day battle had claimed 401 lives of the 32nd Division and 6,700 of the Japanese forces.

Greene relates another event in Luzon. At about 3:00 A.M., a Japanese soldier threw a hand grenade into a foxhole with two Americans in it. One was killed and the other severely wounded. The man who was killed, Bob Wheezer, had served forty months in the war and was scheduled to be sent home in nine to twelve hours. Greene relates this story to illustrate how a few hours can literally make the difference between life and death, when it comes to war.

Word came that the Japanese had surrendered and the war was over. It took days and even weeks for all the Japanese soldiers to get the word and surrender. Whayland says that when the war was over, the "Japs" became "Japanese soldiers." He compliments them as being "well-disciplined, well-trained, brave soldiers who were undersupplied." General Yamashita, who was to the Japanese what Gen. Douglas MacArthur was to the Americans, surrendered to their division, but not to Greene's regiment.

The thought prevailed that now that the war was over, the Americans would get to go home in a few days, but that was not the case for Greene's unit. They were chosen to be the occupational forces in Japan. Shortly after landing in Japan, Greene had earned enough points to get out of the Army and go home. Although he was offered another stripe with the rank of tech sergeant, he chose to go home.

The first year Greene was home, every few weeks he suffered from chills and fever, signs that the malaria was coming back. The entire time he was in the Army, he had taken two little yellow pills every day to ward off the disease and had returned from the war a very distinctive color of yellow.

According to two books written by Greene, entitled *Why Are You So Yellow* and *Grateful Soldier . . . Not Great Soldier,* the American POW death rate for those men held in German POW camps was 1.3 percent, while the rate for those men held in Japanese camps was 45 percent. He notes that according to the Japanese War Crimes Trials Records, the plan was to execute all POWs if it appeared that the Japanese would lose the war. The war ended so abruptly, however, that their plan couldn't be carried out. He also says that in the two years he was overseas, he never once heard anyone call them Japanese. "Japs" was the worst thing Americans could think of to call the race who had perpetrated so much pain and death.

Greene also notes in his books that documents entitled "Historian Details Horrors of WWII Cannibalism" related that whole groups of Japanese soldiers resorted to cannibalism, even when it was not a matter of starvation. In some cases, Japanese "officers ordered troops to eat human flesh to give them a 'feeling of Victory.'"

Greene offers a special tribute to all the nurses who attended to the wounded and dying during the war. For many, they were the hope the soldiers needed to survive. For others, it meant someone to be with them in their last moments.

The 32nd Division was awarded 10,812 Purple Hearts during the war.

Fifty Years Later: Whayland H. Greene, left, James Valentine, center, and Charles Dunnam, right.

Odus L. Felts, February 1950, Okinawa.

Odus L. Felts

1st. Lt. 0961639
Master Sergeant RA 35112924
53rd Armored Engineer Battalion, Part of the
8th Armored Division Headquarters

I was born on April 14, 1920, in Arlington, Kentucky. After completing high school, I attended Murray State Teacher's College, Murray, Kentucky, for one year until enlisting in the Army in April 1942, shortly after Pearl Harbor was bombed by Japan on December 7, 1941.

I was assigned to the 53rd Armored Engineer Battalion, a part of the 8th Armored Division, where I received basic military training and later trained overseas replacements for combat. My speciality was combat demolitions, land, and personnel mines, booby traps, and building roads and bridges to include pontoon and steel. I also laid and cleared minefields. My initial pay was $21 per month. I was promoted to master sergeant and sergeant major of the battalion, then division.

We were ordered overseas (Europe) for combat and fought approximately 600 miles from LaHavre, France, to Salzburg, Austria, crossing France, Belgium, and Germany, doing mostly what we were trained to, only under real circumstances. On one occasion, I did not get a shower for six months. We were outside and constantly on the move. We did, however, get new socks weekly.

Dachau Death Camp

On the day we liberated Dachau, I recall a combat engineer captain, a jeep driver, and I were working with the infantry. This was not unusual, because we did reconnaissance, clearing and laying land mines and building bridges and roads so the other combat troops could keep on the move. I remember building a platoon bridge across the Danube River (I believe that was the name of the river), two or three times. Each time, the Germans lobbed a mortar shell in the center of it and watched it float downstream.

We saw what appeared to be a small, clean village with a plant or factory and a railroad yard with several boxcars, on the sidings or tracks. As we progressed, we discovered what the plant really was. The boxcars were loaded with bodies and skin-covered skeletons. Very few were alive, existing in their own waste. Some were naked, others wearing striped pajamas. There were several crematories and gas chambers, and stacks of clothing lying around. Bodies were stacked like cordwood next in line for the crematories.

The odor of human waste, filth, and singed flesh was sickening. We were ordered back to our unit bivouac area. We were then followed by the medics and burial units. We arrived in our bivouac area, ate our C-rations, and shortly afterward were strafed by the German air force. The next day while on reconnaissance, we were ambushed. My machine gunner was killed, as were some of the men in the back. I manned the gun and we fought our way out. I was lucky. I only had some bullet holes in my pant legs, but was not wounded.

On another occasion, we were securing an area which included a farmhouse. A small child was standing in the front yard waving a white flag, but when we got within range, the house contained a machine gun nest and they opened fire. Several soldiers on both sides were killed. It was a costly lesson for us all.

After the war in Europe, we were returned to the United States for furloughs and then boarded landing craft ships for the invasion of Japan proper. The atomic bomb was dropped. Japan surrendered. I later learned that the Army had 100 percent replacements for us. They anticipated we would all be killed or wounded.

I was overseas more than three and a half years during World War II. I also served in Okinawa, and then, during the Korean War, served in Europe and the Far East. I was awarded a commission and served as an officer. My major assignments were engineer company commander, adjutants of battalions, and assistant adjutants of post and divisions.

I was awarded the Award of the Army Commendation Ribbon, Bronze Star Medal, Good Conduct Medal, American Defense Medal, Victory Medal, Occupation Ribbon (ETS & FEC), EAME Campaign Ribbon with two campaign stars, and Unit Citation.

Odus L. Felts, 2001

Claude V. (Bud) Laws, taken at a coin-operated photo machine in Nancy, France, 1945.

Claude V. (Bud) Laws

79th Division, 314th Infantry Regiment, Cannon Company
1st Division, 18th Infantry Regiment, Cannon Company

I was born in Yakima, Washington, on December 14, 1925. On April 28, 1944, I was inducted into the Army in Fort Lewis, Washington, and sent in May to Camp Roberts, California, where I received training to become a radio operator in the artillery. We were informed that this was an elite group, that the training would be tough, and to expect a 50 percent dropout rate. They were correct on both counts.

At the end of our training at Camp Roberts, we finished by having a two-week intensive field-training course at Hunter Leggett. During that time, we stayed in two-man pup tents. The area was dry and barren, and the ground was full of holes. The first night in the tent wasn't too bad until I threw my covers off in the morning and discovered a tarantula curled up next to me. I exited the tent through an unopened end and took the tent with me. I had never seen a tarantula before and didn't recall ever hearing anything about them. He was one ugly spider!

I found out that all the holes in the ground were made by tarantulas. One of the fellows who was not afraid of spiders carried a tarantula around on a stick. He liked to chase me with it. I got even when I found out he didn't like snakes. I found a fairly large nonpoisonous one and carried it in my pocket. When he would come after me with his spider, I would pull out the snake and we had a Mexican standoff. We soon discarded both our pets.

113

On September 10, 1944, I arrived in Camp Van Dorn, Mississippi. Van Dorn consisted of temporary wooden barracks covered with tarpaper, surrounded by mud. The weather was lousy and we got four inches of snow in one day. So much for the sunny South I was expecting. The training was not nearly as tough as what I had already been through. The worst part was the bad weather and poor living conditions. The barracks each had a wood- or coal-burning potbelly stove in the center of the aisle that ran the length of the building. There were rows of double-high bunks on each side of the aisle.

One day, there was only a few minutes' notice that there was to be a surprise inspection. They were looking for stolen ammunition and explosives. Our stove was cherry red, and one of the guys dumped about 100 rounds of carbine ammunition into the stove. It sounded like a bunch of firecrackers going off. Although none of the ammunition pierced the stove, it looked like it had a bad case of the hives, with bumps all over it. Sometime later, a fellow from an adjoining barracks came in the door acting as if he was drunk and said, "Hey fellows. Look what I found!" He then pulled out a hand grenade, pulled the pin, and rolled it down the aisle. We tipped over beds, trying to find cover. It turned out he had removed the powder and only the firing cap was intact. He was on our list after that.

On December 22, 1944, we boarded a British ship in Boston called the *Aquitania*. It was a luxury liner prior to World War I and then became a troop ship in World War I and World War II. Our group became MPs for the trip. We enforced blackout conditions by night and watched for submarines by day. We were chased by two subs on the way over.

We traveled without convoy, and on December 25, 1944, we were in the middle of the Atlantic for Christmas. Chow line went past the officers' mess, where they were having turkey dinner. There were four to a table (with white tablecloths), and there were some nurses and civilians seated. We went into our chow line and received, among other things, two shriveled-up pork chops that were inedible. They still had ice crystals in them. We also got a box from the Red Cross containing cookies, candies, and other things. This was our Christmas dinner. We received two meals a day, none of which were any good.

On January 1, 1945, we went ashore at LeHavre, France. They took all our equipment and duffel bags and gave us each a spoon, which we tucked into our boots, and a steel helmet, which served as mess gear, among other things. We stayed a couple or three days there and spent our time in a carved-out enclosure in a stone wall, meant for horses and buggies in an old fort. It had no heat nor ventilation.

Next we boarded a train and stayed in a boxcar with straw on the floor. We headed south, where we made a stop in Paris for a few hours. Several French girls came out and gave us bread and cold cuts, the best meal I had eaten since leaving the United States.

From there we continued south, heading for Fontainebleau, where we transferred to open two half-ton trucks. The trip was miserable at best. It was extremely cold, and we were not dressed for the climate. When we would stop for breaks, we would take a coffee can filled with gravel and siphon gas into the can. We would light that on fire and huddle around it to try to stay warm. We traveled approximately 200 miles in this manner to an area that reminded me of Switzerland. It had chateaux build on the hillside that were equipped with steam radiators that were very welcome.

At this point we all split up. I went with a fellow by the name of Henry Ford to Bischwiller, France, and became a member of the 314th Infantry Regiment, Cannon Company, and the 79th Division. This was approximately early to mid-January, 1945.

Neither Henry nor I realized that we had come into the division during one of the major battles. We had no idea as to what we were supposed to do or why we were there. We spent the first night in an upstairs bedroom of the command post, only to find out the next morning that the side of the wall had been hit during the night before with artillery fire. That explained why the other two fellows in the room slept on the floor near an interior wall.

The next morning we were told to go out, dig a foxhole, and make a home. It was here I learned that when you hear a shell go over, you don't stick your head up to see where it lands. I did that only once. You also don't stand outside looking at a ME109 fighter plane to see what everyone was shooting at. They were flying at about telephone pole height. The bullets and anti-aircraft shrapnel were coming down like rain.

We were chased out of this location by German panzer tanks. My first view of a panzer tank was when I was sitting in a two-hole outhouse and had the front wall blown off.

After leaving Nancy, France, we headed north with our new trucks and equipment. We went up past Luxembourg into Belgium and joined General Patton's army. We received orders to scrape the mud off our boots and polish them to a high shine, and to take the camouflage netting off our steel helmets. Then we turned our helmets in to receive a shiny coat of green paint, which made them look like mirrors.

We dug in just outside an orchard on a hillside. While we were in our foxholes, Patton's tanks pulled right in over our foxholes, stopped and fired a few rounds at the Germans on the other side of the valley, then left. We got hit by all of the artillery shells aimed at the tanks. By this time, we did not care too much for General Patton.

From Belgium we were moved to Hoenbroek, Holland. We moved into position next to the Rhine River. Gunfire went off all night. Our artillery was firing continuous barrages across the river into Germany. Airplanes were making continuous round-trip flights, dropping bombs in the area we were going to. We counted more than 200 airbursts over our heads from our own artillery, and we were nearly hit by a load of bombs dropped prematurely by one of our own planes. We saw several of our aircraft get shot down.

During the first part of March, sometime around midnight, we moved across the Rhine. We traveled on a barge that held our truck with a cannon behind it and some other supplies. I looked up to see a German plane strafing the river. They had white tracers and were moving a path straight toward our barge. Sergeant Popovic did not know how to swim and hollered that he would guarantee a medal to anyone who would fish him out of the water. Fortunately, just before they got as far as our barrage, they quit shooting and pulled up. When the plane was right over our heads, an anti-aircraft shell hit it right in the belly. The plane blew up.

We moved to a new position where several planes had been shot down. One was an American plane full of paratroopers that crashed and burned with all aboard.

Others were British planes that had crashed in the area. Most of us were sick enough to our stomachs after that view that we didn't feel like eating for about a week.

We moved up to another position alongside a raised railroad track. We were there for a few days and had all kinds of excitement. One night there was an artillery barrage with airbursts. The next morning one of the fellows in the company raised his head up to get out of his foxhole and his nose hit something sharp. He took a flashlight to investigate. A sharp piece of shrapnel had come through the dirt and the wood over his foxhole and had stopped about two inches from his nose. From then on until the war was over, when we moved into position, that fellow never stopped digging. He dug down as far as he could and threw the dirt out. Then he would start at one end of the foxhole and dig down and throw the dirt out the upper end. Sometimes he'd be down there three layers before he'd quit. It scared the daylights out of him.

By Easter, we were in Duisburg, Germany, in a small farmhouse. A jeep pulled up out front and a commanding officer came inside. All of a sudden there was a big blast and the house shook. We all dove for the basement floor. It turned out that the jeep driver had several hand grenades hanging from the dash. The pin had come out of one of them, causing them all to explode. The jeep looked like a sieve.

Shortly after that, we moved up to a town called Mengede. Six of us quartered in a nice little stucco house. I was inside with the blinds closed. A mortar shell went off just outside the front door. I ran out to see what happened and where it had come from. A young boy, maybe ten or twelve years old, came out from behind the fence with his hand blown off. He had found the mortar and the mortar shells, and had decided to try to hit us. He almost did. I got the company medic to take him into the field hospital.

After the Germans surrendered, the British army was to take over the area that we were occupying. We were to go down to Czechoslovakia for handling of additional displaced persons. We were guarding the Russian/American zone like. We didn't do much of anything except shoot back and forth across the line all night long. The Czechs didn't like us because we were going with their girl friends. We were fair game. Nobody was supposed to be out. Of course, we all went out. Occasionally, we were shot at.

The last night we were in Czechoslovakia, the company had a big party. The company commander had received a tip that a large group of displaced persons was planning to raid a nearby farm, with the intention of killing everyone and destroying the buildings. He assigned one other man and me to guard the farm. I had a carbine and a radio, and the other fellow had a BAR (Browning automatic rifle). We were to call in to the company every half-hour with a status report. This worked fine for the first couple of hours, and then we could no longer raise anybody on the company radio. We decided that there wasn't a heck of a lot two of us could do against a hundred or so DPs, so we lay down on the floor upstairs and went to sleep. They had apparently found out that the farm was being guarded and never showed up. The day we got back to the company, they had left us about a teaspoonful of champagne apiece, to show us what it tasted like.

The next day, while on a three-day pass to Paris, the bomb was dropped on Hiroshima. It was pretty exciting. All the headlines were in French, but you could still tell, basically, what it was and what had happened. From Czechoslovakia, we were moved to Dalherda, Germany, to guard a POW camp.

From there, we were getting ready to go back to the States when the war ended in Japan. That was the end of my trip back to the States. I was placed in the 1st Infantry Division. Somewhere near Nurnberg at Windsheim, I joined up with the 1st and became a switchboard operator with Cannon Company, 18th Infantry Regiment. Then I became a radio chief and got my T5 rating. I was actually acting as communications sergeant. It was written on my discharge as communications sergeant for MOS. However, my rating was frozen. I wouldn't be there long enough to get any advancement, so I stayed as a T5.

From Windsheim, we went to Coburg, Amberg, Bamberg, and Reginsburg. One morning I got up and found my name was on the bulletin board. It showed that I was to be shipped home the next day. I left all my equipment to be divided up among my friends, packed all my other clothes in a duffel bag, and left for Bremerhaven. That was May 20, 1946. The boat we left on was a liberty ship, and we were in the worst storm of the Atlantic for that year. I arrived back at the States and was discharged on June 4, 1946. On that day, I joined the reserves and spent seven years altogether with them.

During my service time, I earned a Combat Infantryman's Badge, a Victory Medal, an Army of Occupation Medal, a Good Conduct Medal, and the European African Middle Eastern Service Medal with two battle stars. Our regiment won two French Croix de Guerres, a red one and a green one.

Bud Laws, 1999

CSM John F. Bednarczyk (Ret.)

John F. Bednarczyk

CSM, Ret.
16th Regiment, 1st Infantry Division, Company H
A.T. Company Guard Duty, Rosenheim, Germany
1st Squadron, 2nd Con Squadron, clerk M.P. Section S-2,
Augsburg, Germany
1/69th Armor 25th infantry Division S-2 Sgt., Hawaii
1st Bde, 2nd Armd Division, S-2 Sgt, Fort Hood, Texas
1/10 Cav. 4th Infantry Division-CSM, Vietnam

In 1945, I was inducted into the Army at Fort Sheridan, Illinois, received basic training at Camp Fannin, Texas, then was shipped to Camp Drum, New York. From there I went overseas to Rosenheim, Germany.

During our first three days out of the New York port, we had to return, as three liberty ships had cracked hulls. We escorted them back to port. The storms were so severe, even the old sailors were seasick. The ship smelled so bad they had to swab it down with creosote. There were 5,000 troops on a converted German luxury liner, captured when the war started. When we went through the English Channel, sailors were shooting at floating mines in the channel, in order to explode them.

Once we reached Rosenheim, I was put in the 16th Regiment, 1st Infantry, A.T. Company Guard Duty.

From 1945 to 1946, I was stationed in Bamberg and Ansbach, Germany, then sent to Copenhagen, Denmark, on R&R. Later in 1946, I was in Passau, Germany, where I served

121

MP Duty along the Austrian border, to prevent smuggling on the Danube River. Black market was the point into Hungary.

One night after pulling guard duty on CID house, as I returned to the barracks, duty sergeant got ahold of me, as the fellow who took my shift had shot himself with a .45 pistol, through the leg. (He had come over with me on the same ship.) I had to finish his tour. We were guarding the house because three CID agents had been killed by smugglers.

During this period, there was a great exit of the Sudetenland, Deutsche, from Czechoslovakia into Passau, Germany.

I returned to Landshut, Germany, where I served as an interpreter in Polish for displaced personnel from Eastern Europe, Russia, and Poland. It was a tent city until movement to countries which took them. Our unit stood guard at the railroad. I was present at the Nürnberg Trial and met some of the Russian soldiers. I went on R&R to Rome, Italy, through Paris, France; Switzerland; and Milan, Italy, where Mussolini was hanged.

From 1946 to May 1947, I continued to serve in Company H, 16th Infantry, 1st Division, in Salzburg, Austria. My job was to guard the railroad yards, the stockade, the Hungarian Crown Jewels, and the dependent quarters of the first dependents to be sent overseas. I was also a border guard between Austria and Germany.

In 1947, I was sent from there back to the States and discharged at Fort Sheridan, Illinois. After working on the BO Railroad and returning home to the wheat fields of Nebraska, by buddy and I enlisted again. Zweibrucken, Germany, was my next destination, for clerk typist school. In Augsburg, Germany, I was in the 1st Squadron 2nd Constabulary Squadron as a clerk MP Section S-2. From 1948 to 1952 I went to Intelligence School in Garmisch, Germany. The unit I was in became 1st Bn, 2nd Armed Cav. Regiment, Company B. I also received training at the French Zone, Munsingen, Germany.

From 1952 to 1953, my assignment was border duty for the East-West Zone, Arzberg, Germany for three months of rotating duty, maneuvers, and monthly alerts. We were the blocking force for Fulda Gap. I became an S-2 sergeant for 1st Bn, 2nd Armed Cav. Regt., then an aerial observer, where I flew in a fixed-wing Piper Cub along the border.

From 1954 to 1961, I worked in various other assignments. From 1961 to 1964. We were training for duty in Vietnam. Every Saturday morning was a full-field layout. We endured jungle training, repelling from helicopters and cliffs, rope descent over lakes, monkey rope crossing on rope, had to eat food found in the jungle, and walk five miles with machine guns and mortars.

Other extensive training in Vietnam, Germany, and the Mojave Desert filled the years until 1967. In 1968 I was discharged from the military.

John F. Bednarczyk, 2000

Farris Ivie

Farris Ivie

158th Regimental Combat Team
"The Bushmasters"

I was born in Forest, Texas, in December 1917. Upon completing high school, I went to Texas A&M University. While there, I took a civil service exam just for fun, to see if I could pass it. I did and was sent to Washington, D.C., to work in the Commerce Department doing the census. While I was there, on December 7, 1941, Pearl Harbor was attacked.

Orders came for me to report to Camp Wheeler, Georgia on February 2, 1942, where I was to be trained as a replacement for troops overseas, either in the European or the Pacific theaters. They told us to bring warm clothes and a big overcoat. We were trained for almost a year in jungle fighting in a unit called the Bushmasters. The bushmaster is the largest and most poisonous snake anywhere in the Americas. Our shoulder patch was a machete with a snake wrapped around it.

The Pacific was the destination for the 158th Infantry Regiment. We were a combat team, with our own transportation, trucks, artillery, and medic outfits.

After landing at Brisbane, Australia, we were sent up into the hills about twenty or thirty miles where mosquitoes nearly ate us alive. The Japs were getting too close, so we were sent to Port Moresby, New Guinea. It was the beginning of 1943. Our next stop was Goodenough Island, then on to New Britain Island, where our 2nd Battalion was on PT Boats, and once we reached the island, that was where we made camp. During a fierce air raid, a boy from Fort Worth, Texas, got both of his legs blown off. I picked him up and carried him to a hospital. About two weeks later, the doctors told him he didn't have any legs. He asked them about his sex life, and they told him that was all right. Some time later, he visited me in Carthage. He went on to work in the legislature but soon after was killed chasing another man's wife.

While in New Britain, the fighting was fierce. I heard a shot go right over my head, so I fell down and didn't move for over two hours because I knew the sniper was still out there and had me in his sights. Finally, I eased out of there, right into the arms of my buddy Whitten, who hugged me and started crying. He thought the Japs had killed me.

At Sarmi on the mainland of New Guinea, we saw some rough fighting. We thought it was an army of about 5,000 men, but later found out it was over 55,000. For twenty-five days, we didn't change our socks. The Japanese were so close to us that when one of the officers was shot, his sword fell in the hole with us. It had a pearl handle and was really fancy. I kept it as a souvenir until someone stole it out of my bag on the way home.

As our men were attempting to bury the dead Japs, they decided to bring in a bulldozer, dig one big hole, and pull the bodies into it by putting piano wire around their bodies and dragging them into the hole. But a couple of boys went out there and said, "Let us show you how do do that." They would get a pickax and stick it in their stomachs and drag them over into the hole.

At Noemfoor Island, we lost 170 men and over 3,000 Japs were killed. It was a massacre. We took the island so the B-29s could take off and go to Tokyo and back, and wouldn't have to refuel in midair. From Noemfoor, we went to the Philippines, were we connected up with the 42nd Division. We got the Presidential Citation for capturing some really big guns and enduring some rough fighting.

Some of our men volunteered to go in and take over a camp where American prisoners were being held, dating back since early 1942, when they were forced to walk up north of Luzon from Bataan, with nothing to eat. The walk was called the Bataan Death March. One of my friends from Houston volunteered to attempt the rescue. He was given no guns nor any type of weapons, only a knife. Our men would sneak up behind the guards, wrap wire around their throats real fast, and stab them with the knife before the guard could make a sound. One by one they knocked off the guards.

Our men were in bad shape. This was one of the worst things. I hope I never see this again. I was slightly wounded and received the Combat Infantry Badge. Suffering from tropical malaria, and pretty shook up, I wasn't really myself when we got out of there.

We saw a lot of action while in the Philippines. At Batangas, in the Catholic church, we saw where sometime back, the Japs had rounded up all the people in the town, herded them into the church, blocked them from getting out, and murdered every one of them. The Filipinos really hated the Japs.

We landed at Legaspi, the south end of Luzon, on April 1, 1945. Up until now, my folks had not been allowed to know where I was. One night some of our friends were listening to the radio and the news announcer said, "Captain Farris Ivie had led his troops ashore at Legaspi on southern Luzon, and moved north to wipe out the Japanese that were there." They called my folks and told them where I was. My kid brother was also shipped to the Philippines at the end of the war, but we never knew where each other was until we got back home. I was still in Luzon when the war ended. We thought we were going to get to go home but were instead sent to Japan as part of the occupation force. Landing at Yokohama, then going through Tokyo, we saw what destruction the B-29s had done. Only crumpled brick and tin remained. The city was really torn up.

When we finally were sent home, I arrived with a temperature of 105 degrees. I had tropical malaria. When it continued to get worse, to the point that I was passing out, they packed me in a big vat filled with ice. My temperature had risen to 108 degrees. In December of 1945, once I was better, my folks came to San Antonio to get me.

I married in January 1946 and eventually settled in Carthage, Texas, where I have been ever since.

At the war's end, I was the commander of a rifle company in the Philippines which began with 5 officers and 792 men and ended with 1 officer and 52 men.

Jack Harris, 1940s.

Jack A. Harris

"The Night Raiders"
D-Day Invasion-June 6, 1944-Omaha Beach
29th Division, U. S. Army

I was born in Beckville, Texas, and joined the Army in 1943 at the age of sixteen, but my birth record said seventeen. I volunteered to be a paratrooper for a special unit that required being six feet tall and weighing between 2.5 and 3.5 pounds per inch. This was an elite battalion. I made platoon sergeant two weeks after joining. My rank was staff sergeant.

We were shipped straight to England for training, where we also learned some of the German language, to help us communicate. We were training in the English Channel, not knowing whether we would go over by boat or air. On one of the maneuvers, we ran into a German E-boat and lost 800 of our men. Only four years ago did the Army finally admit this had happened. The Army threatened us, if we ever spoke about it. They covered it up. They knew the invasion of D-Day was coming, so they kept the men's names on the roster. Then on D-Day they took two-thirds of them out like they had been killed in the invasion of France. They phased the rest of them out a week later, until finally the whole 800 were written off. Then, about four years ago, the government admitted they lost these men to the German E-boats.

We trained up until just before D-Day. There is a picture of me in the English Channel on a landing craft infantry boat on D-Day. The front end of the boat has ramps which let down and

129

was supposed to run up on the beach. However, the Germans were defending the beach, so we couldn't run up near the beach. The boats let us off way out in the water, and then we had to wade to the beach. When we did, and if we got there, we knew most of the other guys had gotten killed at Omaha Beach. That's where we landed on D-Day. A lot of mistakes were made on that day, and our pack was a big one. They had equipment all up top in the pack like bandoliers of ammunition. We each had a belt around our waist which stayed on with the pack harness over it. The belt had a cylinder in it. If we jumped out in the water over our heads, we squeezed the belt buckle and it punched the cylinder and inflated our belt like it was a life preserver. The problem here was that we were top-heavy. Once we inflated those belts, our heads went down and feet went up with all that equipment. We couldn't get out of it and were going to drown! I saw hundreds of men floating out across there in the water with their feet up. Of course, I saw what was happening and didn't inflate mine.

I have a friend named Jim Slaughter who claims he was the first man wounded on D-Day. This was portrayed in the movie *Saving Private Ryan* and in *The Longest Day*. They sent me a tape of the first one before they released it and wanted me to comment on it. He was a personal friend of mine. The Germans were really blasting away at us coming and going. He got shot right before he got to the seawall beyond the beach. They were killing men by the dozens. In all the confusion, who knows for sure. But if he wants to claim he was the first, it's all right with me.

Luckily, I didn't get a scratch there. I was with the 29th Division, but I was with the Night Raiders. We were a special unit attached with the 29th.We were similar to the Rangers but were better trained. We were the best-trained unit in the whole United States Army according to Gen. Omar Bradley. It was Bradley's idea to create the Night Raiders.

Taking out the Germans' big guns covering the beach was our job on D-Day. Although we lost a lot of men, we were successful in our objective. General Eisenhower came in the next day and was amazed that of the entire beach, there was not a place to put your foot without stepping on a dead man. When the tide went out, it took some of them out to sea. Many of the men who were wounded and fell were hit again and killed simply because of the constant firing. Because of this, the ratio that day was that for six or seven wounded, one lived.

We had come in with 220 men and at first count had 39. We had a 82 percent casualty rate. It was a sad day. I lost so many of my friends with whom I had trained for the last thirteen months. After that, they sent us replacements. We'd lose most of them the same day we got them, or the next.

Just after the Battle of the Bulge, while we were still in Germany, I was on another mission. I hit the ground from my jump after leaving the plane. I knew I was in trouble before I hit the ground, because I saw the Germans shooting at us as we were coming down. I unbuckled everything and got ready so I could get it all off as quickly as I landed. I did that but hit the ground within a few feet of a German machine gun. He was dug in the middle of the street with a net thrown over it for camouflage. I didn't see it until he started shooting.

I had a Thompson submachine gun on a strap. I got it ready to use on the group and was headed toward that machine gun nest but didn't know he was there. He was watching me all the time, and what he was waiting for was that I had about five men about half a block in back of me. He saw them, too, and hoped I wouldn't run over him before they caught up to me so he could shoot us all. But he saw that I was just gonna keep coming. He fired, and the first shot hit my arm and busted it, as well as hitting the Thompson submachine gun. I had a funny sensation. I looked around me and saw the gun shooting up the street. The bullets sped out, for it was a German MG-42. I had a .45 pistol. By now, I'd seen him, so I headed for the machine gun with my pistol in hand, firing as I went. Fortunately for me, I hit the gunner, I guess, with the first shot. Instead of knocking him backward, he fell over the gun. That was lucky for me, for that gesture fixed it so that the other four men couldn't get the gun. I kept coming and shooting and just dived into the hole when I got there, but I had been shot in the arms and both legs. I was really hurt bad.

My men yelled, asking how bad I was hurt, then they came and got me out of the hole. The Germans decided to make a break for it. A couple of them got away from the machine gun nest. They ran around the corner, then came back shooting at us. They hit all these other men and knocked them all down. Now we were all down, and they just kept coming. They were on the attack now, coming through the little town. They thought we were all dead, so they just bypassed us to meet another, larger group.

We eventually found a cellar and pulled the dead and wounded inside. One or two were already dead, and two died later, leaving only another guy and me. He was wounded but only had flesh wounds. No broken bones. We stayed there for three days and nights, until some English soldiers found us and I was taken to an English hospital in Birmingham, England. I stayed there for almost a year. The war was over for me.

When the war ended, I had fought all across Western Europe, including France, Belgium, Luxembourg, Holland, and Germany. My highest combat decoration was the Distinguished Service Cross (DSC). We were in France when I wiped out a German command post of nine by myself. I also received their Croix de Guerre, which is their highest medal. In England, I was given their Military Order of Merit medal. It's also a high decoration, equivalent to our Silver Star. To get this medal, you have to put your life on the line, and it has to be under fire. I was awarded three Silver Star decorations from the U.S. Army. I won the first one in France just after the D-Day invasion. Then I got one for action near Brest, France, and the last one in Germany. I received three Purple Heart medals for wounds in action. I had made five combat jumps on paratrooper assignments. The first time I was wounded was in Germany, the second was with the SS troops and the machine gun nest, and the third was on July 12, at St. Lo in France, I think.

I was also given a "Battle Field Commission" to the rank of first lieutenant, which is a recognition for leadership. This was just before D-Day. The company commander was killed, and we only had four second lieutenants as officers in the company. They had just arrived and hadn't really been trained right. So General Bradley asked me if I'd lead the company. I said, "Well, hey, General, I had every intention of doing so." You know I was saying that as a joke. He made me first lieutenant and the company commander. However, I got wounded on July 12, 1944. When I got back to the hospital, I resigned my commission and went back to being first sergeant. I liked the job better, and the pay was better for me, too.

When I was in the Night Raiders, we often went days without sleeping or eating. Once, I went forty-two days without changing socks or pulling off my shirt. After forty-two days they could probably smell me before they could see me. When I returned home from the war in February 1946, I was still a teenager. I wasn't twenty yet.

When I got home, I returned to the farm. In 1953, I went into the ministry. I'm now seventy-two, and I've been trying to retire since I was sixty-five. I've preached in all fifty states and abroad. I've preached hundreds of weddings and funerals, and taught lots of seminars and held revivals all over the country.

The experiences of World War II and of what I went through will never leave me. I'm still restless and nervous at night. I think it goes back to when our sleeping patterns were torn up by combat. Once in a while I'll have a flashback in my sleep. I'll be back there, and it's so real. It's just like it was. My wife can calm me down. It just never leaves me. I think about the combat experiences. That's part of me.

Below is a story I wrote about a friend of mine.

The Third Man
A Story About a Hero WWII
"The third man of the third squad of the third platoon of the third battalion"

He was a young man from Texas who came as a replacement to our company. He was nineteen years old and just out of basic training. He was assigned to be the "third rifleman of the third squad of the third platoon of the third battalion." He was destined to twelve days' combat in the infantry front lines.

The first night he spent in a foxhole with a buddy. The enemy threw in a royal barrage of artillery shells. The third man was scared more than he had ever been, and in the next twelve days, he would witness and experience twenty-four more nerve-racking than the last. He would see 100 men from his company killed. He would attack twelve times in the face of MG fire, rifle fire, tank and mortar fire. He would wade through 200 dead enemy soldiers. Half these days, no food rations would make it through. His stomach growled from hunger pangs. He just kept fighting.

He saw eight strong, brave, trained men go berserk. They all had one thing in common. They had to run. They lost all sense of direction. Four of these ran the wrong direction, and they were no more. Four were subdued by their buddies and pointed the right direction. They would get help back at the rear. Some would recover, but for some, every time they hear a sudden loud noise—it would start over for them. But the third man kept fighting.

He went on three patrols out in no man's land at night. His heart beat so loudly, he was sure the enemy would hear it and his position would be revealed. He saw two of his buddies killed while on patrol.

He attacked across open fields under smokescreens. He never complained. He just kept fighting. The weather was cold and wet. He would freeze at night and thaw out in the daytime. He often thought of home, his family, and his high school sweetheart. She said she would wait no matter how long it took. He would write her every night. He was so happy when our mail would catch up to us and he could mail the ones he had written to her.

Now came the twelfth day. It started with our attack, as did most other days. We threw out a smokescreen because the field ahead was open. We called for artillery to be fired three hundred yards ahead of our position. Now came the fifteen-minute barrage, and we moved forward. The enemy threw a barrage at us. The field was still filled with smoke. We made some progress, suffering rather heavy casualties. Then came time to dig in and hold our newly captured position.

At this time, our mail clerk caught up to us with a bag of mail. He hand-delivered to our foxholes. The third man received two letters, as did his buddy. He began by reading first the letter from his mother. He was very happy as he read that his three sisters were now all teenagers and all was well, or would be when he returned from that awful war.

Letter number two was from his sweetheart. She told of her love and devotion to him and that she waited with longing for his return. She hoped they could be married real soon when he returned. Then, he looked over at his buddy, expecting to see a happy man, only to see him in tears. He inquired. His buddy handed his letter over. It was a "Dear John" letter. She had met someone and fallen in love. She didn't plan it this way, but it just happened. She hoped he would understand and forgive. She still hoped the best for him and would continue to pray for his safety. This was good-bye, from Lucy.

Now we were facing the enemy at about three hundred yards. Night was coming on and we did as usual under these circumstances. We sent out an outpost of two men, "the third man of the third squad of the third platoon of the third battalion" and his buddy. The two had trained together in the States and had come to us as a pair. They went out about one hundred fifty yards, dug in, and remained alert. They were in touch with the main body by radio. About ten o'clock, things had been very quiet. The "third man" informed us of some kind of activity on the enemy front. Then came the artillery, mortar shells, and we heard tanks. The "third man" told us he saw two tanks slowly approaching his outpost. He requested permission to withdraw to our position. Permission was granted.

The five-minute notice by the "third man" no doubt saved us from being overrun and killed. He now called for artillery one hundred yards from his outpost. The artillery came. They fired another volley. We opened with MG fire. At this time, the enemy evidently called off his surprise attack.

We tried to contact the outpost and could get no response. The "third man" was silent. Our last contact had been 11:30 P.M. on the twelfth day.

Morning came. We attacked. I wanted to pay close attention when

Jack Harris, 2000

we came to that outpost. As we approached, we saw that their position had taken a direct hit by an artillery shell. The "third man of the third squad of the third platoon of the third battalion" and his best friend were no more. But wait. I saw, hanging from an apple tree, strings of human flesh and hair. Just small fragments, here and there.

He was my hero—and here is why. For twelve days in the heat of the battle, all of his human senses told him to throw down his rifle and run, that to continue here was death. Go berserk and run. Save your life.

But the third man just kept fighting. In life he had received no medals nor commendations, but in death he would receive the prestigious Purple Heart. I recommended him for the Silver Star for gallantry in action against the enemy. These would be awarded posthumously.

The rest of the story we leave in the hands of our Creator, our Savior, and Keeper, and Preserver alike, knowing that the Judge of all the earth will do right.

Jack B. Bennett

PFC, 1st Infantry Division,
18th Regiment, 2nd Battalion, Company E

Much has been written about the D-Day invasion of France on June 6, 1944. I was a member of Company E, 2nd Battalion, 18th Regiment of the First Infantry Division and was scheduled to land on a sector known by its code name Easy Red on Omaha Beach in the second wave. It was just as terrible as has been reported many times. Shellfire, noise, and confusion reigned. The noise was especially deafening. The Germans had wonderful equipment and well-fortified positions, and suffered no damage from the Air Force, due to cloud cover. Most of the bombardment from the Navy landed back on the beach proper, because they had no close observation and the rockets, which were to precede the landing of troops, fell short of the beach. I contribute the eventful success of the landing to the youth and determination of the American troops and the lack of depth of the German defenses in the area.

A large number of American men were from eighteen to twenty-four years old, while the German troops were much older and, except for the division that was moved in at the last minute, were not German, but troops captured from occupied countries under the command of German noncommissioned and commissioned officers for absolute control.

The main dominating feature of Omaha Beach is the cliff in the back of the beach proper. This cliff, which I believe is

Jack B. Bennett, England, 1944.

about 250 feet high, was heavily fortified with underground trenches and living quarters for the German troops. All above ground was open trenches as well as mortar and machine gun placements, and much of the area was heavily mined.

There were about five exits or small valleys leading from the beach proper, which were designated E1, E2, etc. These draws, when cleared, were to become roads for tanks, trucks, etc. to exit up the cliff. Our mission was to clear E1 and E2 because it had not been cleared by the initial assault teams. The exits were dominated by two large concrete "pillboxes." One was just above the water line. The other about midway up the cliff, protecting the draw from the infiltration off the beach.

When we landed in the second wave about 9:30 A.M., it appeared as if nothing had been accomplished, and few, if any, other troops had landed in this sector. We had mislanded by several hundred yards from our assigned sector, due to tides as well as not enough lanes through the obstacles in the water. Because it was not high tide, most of us jumped into the water, which was at least five feet deep or more. When we stepped into holes, it was over our heads. For all of these reasons, confusion on the beach was almost uncontrollable. All of the German artillery and mortars were presighted and were pounding the beach and the water offshore with great precision. Any vehicle reaching the beach was usually hit.

The men from my company who were not hit immediately began to go up the bluff off the beach proper. Because of the mines and small arms fire, the going was slow, as we had to stay low and line up almost single-file. Many men stepped on mines. In fact, we had to step over and around many on the way up the bluff.

Once we reached the top of the bluff, we started to clean out most of the German troops by capturing them or making them retreat. As I said, the defenses were very shallow, but on top of the bluff we had the hedgerows, which had many mortar, machine guns, retreating riflemen, and 88mm artillery.

Because men getting up the bluff were so scattered, no one knew where anyone else was, so we started out for our assigned objectives in small groups, rather than the way it should have been by company strength. As a consequence, we bypassed many

German troops, but they were also disorganized and just trying to escape from being cut off.

Once we got troops up the bluff, the Germans were in real danger, as they had few fortifications to protect their immediate real area. By about 10:00 P.M., although very scattered, we reached a point near the village of Collyville, which is about one mile inland from the beach. By late afternoon of June 6, D-Day, with the aid of some brave Navy destroyers who came in near shore to give us artillery support, the landing of troops was speeded up and continued throughout the night. We got little rest at the conclusion of a long day of June 6, 1944, nor did we have much to eat. Groups of German troops trying to escape from the beach got into a brief firefight with our men, digging in for the night. More American troops were arriving. By the next morning, we were fairly well organized.

We had cut the road running in back of the beach of Collyville, which had been the objective of the 16th Regiment. The 18th Regiment took over their objective, because they suffered such causalities both wounded and killed in the initial assault of the beach that they were no longer to be an effective unit, although those that did make it to the top of the bluff were of great help to us that night.

And so, for me, began the long road through France, Belgium, and into the edge of Germany. I was wounded for the second time, seriously, in the small German village of Verlutenhider, on the outskirts of the large city of Aachen, which was the northern anchor of the Siegfried line dividing Germany and France, on October 13, 1944.

The following story just proves that sometimes it is amazing just how small the world seems to be. All stories need not be so serious and full of woe. The following one is true and on the lighter side. Many funny things happened during the war, along with the more terrible things.

When I was stationed at Fort Riley, Kansas, in April 1943 for basic training, my executive officer was a first lieutenant named Ganski, who was very tough, but fair. He was strict in military matters and a great instructor. We had several Italian men who came from the Pennsylvania area. One in particular was always falling asleep at Ganski's lectures, training films, and other instructional events. He had a very heavy beard, and even if he shaved in the morning, by noon it looked like he had not shaved at all.

Beards and other facial hair were "no-nos" in 1943, so the soldier was always in trouble, either on KP or guard duty, as punishment by Ganski. Even though he liked the man, he had to keep discipline. The cadre of training NCOs and officers remained in Fort Riley when we shipped out, ready to train the next group, so we assumed we would never see them again.

At the battle of the Falaise Gap, my company was blocking a road to prevent the escape of German infantry, while the Air Force and artillery completely destroyed the trapped Western German Army in France in August in a valley below. Suddenly, we saw a lone German tank approaching. All we had was a 57mm gun, which is like shooting a tank with a BB gun. We fired anyway, and to our amazement, it stopped and the crew surrendered. Within a few minutes, we heard more track vehicles coming toward our position, so we assumed it was more German tanks trying to escape the trap, as there was mass confusion all around.

To our amazement and the point of the story, several half-tracks roared up, all from the 1st Calvary of our division, and standing in the lead half-track, was now *Captain* Ganski, whom we had last seen in Kansas in 1943. He recognized several of us and his first question was, Where was Frank S. Brenski (not his real name), the bearded Italian lad he liked so much in Kansas. We had to tell him that he came with us to the 1st Infantry Division and was in our company, but had been wounded on the beach on D-Day morning, though not seriously.

He thanked us and roared off to war again, and that was the one and only time we ever saw him. To illustrate how much Ganski had liked Frank Brenski during training camp, the lieutenant had violated his own code of an officer by carrying the private to the barracks, as he and the private had had too much to drink on our final night in camp. I have wondered many times if the captain survived the war. I hope that he did, as he was a wonderful training officer. His tough exercises in the morning got us into wonderful physical condition. I have no doubt that it had a great bearing in helping us overcome many

Jack Bennett, 1999

of the terrible physical conditions we met in the first weeks following the invasion and, all things being equal, gave us the advantage on the beach against the odds we faced.

My service lasted from April 2, 1943, until March 26, 1946.

Alexander Russell Bolling, Jr.

94th Infantry Division
WWII Combat, Wounded, Captured, Escaped
Commanded 82nd Airborne Division Forces in Vietnam
Major General, U.S Army

Alexander Bolling was born on September 11, 1922, in Fort McPherson, Georgia. His father was a young captain embarking on a military career. World War II erupted during Bolling's sophomore year at the Untied States Military Academy, and his class chose to forego vacations and other absences from the academy so that it could be graduated in three years. Both military and academic training were intensified. Bolling, already fluent in French, was selected as one of the fifty cadets to learn the German language—a selection which would stand him in good stead less that four years later when he escaped from a German prisoner-of-war camp. On June 1, 1943, Second Lieutenant Bolling graduated from West Point.

Shortly after his arrival at Camp Robinson, he was introduced to Frances Bigbee, the daughter of the vice principal of the Little Rock Senior High School. From the moment of their first meeting, Bud and Fran were together whenever wartime training of his unit was suspended momentarily.

In early 1944, however, the division was transferred to Alabama, and shortly thereafter, Bolling was ordered to proceed

143

Alexander Russell Bolling, Jr., Pentagon duty, 1970.

to a new organization in Mississippi, the 94th Division. The 94th moved north by train to New York City, embarked as an entity (20,000 men) on the British luxury liner *Queen Elizabeth,* and sailed eastward. The ship arrived in Scotland four and a half days later, and the troops were immediately moved by train to southern England. Equipment was drawn. The men and their new equipment were directed aboard landing craft, and by mid-August 1944, the 94th Infantry Division had raced across Omaha Beach and moved into line in Brittany. It had been a rapid trip from the heart of Mississippi to southwestern France.

The fall months were spent containing German units bottled up in the ports of Saint-Nazaire and Lorient. Bud Bolling, an infantry platoon leader, spent much of his time patrolling behind enemy lines and directing fire against targets he had located while on patrol. At one point, while deep in enemy territory, he accidentally encountered some French underground forces, with whom he remained an entire week gathering information. His knowledge of French was of particular value during the period.

When the Battle of the Ardennes occurred in mid-December 1944, Bolling's unit was rushed north to fill one of the gaps created. After bitter fighting in painfully cold weather, the German's advance was stopped, and the 94th Division (in mid-January 1945) began a counteroffensive along the Moselle River, fighting north toward Trier.

The German high command deployed its elite 11th Panzer Division against the 94th. Intense combat was the result, and on January 20, 1945, Lieutenant Bolling was wounded and captured while attempting to reach an isolated infantry company. Bolling was taken to the rear. His wounds were treated with what little medicine the German captors had at the time. He was then evacuated another ten miles, where he was questioned, fed, and given a bed on which to rest.

Shortly after midnight, he managed to escape from his guard, hiding in a snow-filled ditch while his captors searched for him. His freedom was short-lived, however, because a weary German soldier decided to return to the troop area after the search by taking a direct route across the field where Bud was hiding. Shortly thereafter, a frightened Lieutenant Bolling was standing in front of a German colonel wondering what had happened.

Instead of punishing him, the colonel extended the congratulations of the commanding general of the 11th Panzer Division for the young American's demonstration of bravery. He then explained that Bolling would have to be evacuated to the rear more rapidly than anticipated and that this would be punishment enough, because the food was not as plentiful in the rear. At 2:00 A.M., a truck arrived. Bolling was awakened and taken to an isolated farmhouse occupied by a German housewife and her elderly mother. It turned out that the "Hausfrau" had a husband who had been taken prisoner-of-war two years earlier and had been incarcerated in the United States. His letters from America gave such a glowing report of his treatment that the woman and her mother seemed to go out of their way to show their gratitude. Though food was scarce throughout Germany, Lieutenant Bolling was treated to meals of fresh eggs, pork, potatoes, and milk, and the two women took turns throughout the night keeping a small woodstove burning in the kitchen while Bolling slept on the dirt floor.

The comfort ended abruptly on January 22 when Bud was transported to a more standard prison camp north of the Rhine River in the town of Limburg. Because his army serial number gave away the fact that he was a career officer, and because the Germans knew that there was an American division commander in Germany bearing the same name as their new prisoner, he was immediately extracted from the group of prisoners at the camp and taken to a medieval castle in the middle of the town of Diez, just three kilometers away. In this castle was a highly sophisticated interrogation center. The Germans finally gave up on Bolling, and he was returned to the camp at Limburg. Planning for a second escape attempt began. However, just as plans were nearing completion, the entire group of approximately 500 prisoners was marched to the railroad station and placed in railroad boxcars. For five days, the prisoners were kept locked in the boxcars. Once or twice a day, the train would haul, the doors would slide open, and German guards would throw chunks of old cheese into the freezing mass of humanity trapped inside.

On the fifth day, the train arrived at Hammelburg, near Schweinfurt, Germany. Those prisoners who could walk were marched up a hill to a permanent prison camp. Those who had died on the trip were left behind. Those who were critically ill were taken to a dispensary established for that purpose. It was now March 10, and Bud Bolling had not seen a warm room or a decent meal since he left the little farmhouse on top of the hill.

Conditions at Hammelburg were almost as harsh as those at Limburg. Germans who were not at the front had very little food. Blankets were also in short supply, so the prisoners had to sleep huddled together to keep from freezing to death.

On March 27, 1945, after an abortive attempt to reach the camp by a small contingent of General Patton's Army, Bud and three friends managed to escape during the resulting confusion. Two of the friends were too weak to go on and turned back. Eleven days later, after wandering many miles in an attempt to get through the enemy lines, they entered the town of Obervolkach on the Main River, thinking that it had already been captured by advancing American forces. It hadn't, but the town mayor surrendered to Bolling.

With his knowledge of both the French and German languages, Bud located some French prisoners who had worked in the town for almost three years. A provisional French platoon was formed, using confiscated hunting weapons and local bicycles. It was charged with the task of guarding the town until the arrival of American units.

Bud and his companies then went upstairs in the town hall and gorged themselves on the contents of American Red Cross parcels which had somehow managed to reach the French prisoners. They then fell into a deep sleep in immaculately clean beds.

The following morning, on April 8, 1945, American troops from the 42nd Infantry Division were led into town by one of the French prisoners, who had used a confiscated bicycle to find friendly forces. The young lieutenant was processed through administrative channels to the large facilities that had been established to handle prisoners expected to be liberated at the war's end. Because of the length of time he had spent in enemy hands, Bolling was, in accordance with the rules of the Geneva Convention, supposed to be evacuated from the theater of war.

However, he found an opportunity to go north to visit his father, Gen. Alex Bolling, whose troops were in the process of capturing Hannover and who, until this time, had thought his son had been killed in action on January 20.

Bud had lost forty pounds as a prisoner, so General Bolling kept his son at division headquarters for a week to rest and regain his strength. He was then sent down to the front lines, where he became the commander of one of the most frequently committed infantry companies in the division. The war ended without further incident. Bolling and his company finished the conflict on the Elbe River, just thirty miles from Berlin. The unit was then given an area to occupy pending the arrival of trained military government elements.

It was during this period that Bud had an opportunity to repay the kindness of the 11th Panzer Division leaders. With thousands of hungry and disheartened German soldiers fleeing the Russians and attempting to get back to their homes, roadblocks had to be established to screen people pushing westward. Bolling had all soldiers identified as former members of the 11th Panzer Division brought to his command post. There they were told the story of January 20, given cigarettes and food, and thanked personally by a very grateful American officer.

With the creation of zones to be occupied by each of the victorious nations, Bolling's unit was moved south to the vicinity of Heidelberg. Shortly thereafter, Captain (note the promotion) Bolling was ordered to proceed to West Point to become an instructor in the German language. After three years and completion of an intensified course in the Portuguese language, his wife and child moved with him to Brazil, where a second child was born. While in Brazil he completed advanced military training, then served in Taiwan, received a second assignment at West Point, and spent a year at the Army War College. He went on to become an advisor to the Vietnamese army, the Directorate of Operations of the Department of the Army staff in Washington, and three years later was promoted to colonel. In December 1966 he joined the 82nd Airborne Division in North Carolina.

Slightly more than a year after he joined the 82nd, as commanding officer of its 3rd Brigade, Colonel Bolling and his unit were ordered by the president of the United States to fly without delay to Vietnam to assist in countering the enemy threat during the Tet Offensive of February 1968. Bolling, with 4,000 officers and men and all of their equipment, began the 10,000-mile trip within twenty-four hours after receipt of orders from the White House and completed it within ten days.

For the third time, Bud Bolling was back in combat. It wasn't until the summer of 1969 that he was ordered home, after eighteen months of difficult and intense fighting.

Having been promoted while in Vietnam, General Bolling was assigned once again to the Pentagon in Washington, as director of organization for the United States Army. In less than two years, he had received another promotion (to major general) and was sent to Fort Lewis, Washington, to command one of the Army's largest installations.

In 1972, he was ordered once again to Brazil to assume the highest U.S. military post in that country. His familiarity with the language and acquaintanceship with the incumbent Brazilian leaders was probably the reason the army authorities chose to send him there.

In September 1973, after more than thirty-three years in uniform, Bud retired. During his many years of service, he earned two Distinguished Service Medals, three Silver Stars for bravery under fire, three Legions of Merit, two Bronze Stars for valor, eighteen Air Medals, the Purple Heart for wounds received in combat, and numerous other decorations. He was most proud, however, of his parachutist badge and the two combat infantryman's badges, which he often said were the true symbols of his life as a soldier.

Pamela Waddell Bradbury

Pamela Waddell Bradbury

Pearl Harbor, December 7, 1941
Hospital Dietitian
1st Lieutenant upon discharge, 1945

I graduated from the University of Georgia in 1937, with a BS degree in nutrition and institutional management. I also had a twelve-month internship in hospital dietetics from Walter Reed General Hospital in Washington, D.C.

My story of December 7, 1941, is most vivid in my memory, yet I cannot recall what I had for breakfast this morning, as I am eighty-five years old.

On December 6, 1941, my date and I attended a dance at the Royal Hawaiian Hotel in Honolulu. The band from the USS *Arizona* played for us until midnight; consequently, on the morning of December 7, they were allowed to "sleep in" and were all destroyed in the bombing of the *Arizona*. Not one of them survived. That is why I can't bring myself to board the memorial. It is too sacred to me. It grieves me that visitors are so callous and disrespectful, and unpatriotic, as they visit the memorial. It is a shrine and should be treated as such.

On the morning of the bombing, I was "sleeping in," too, as I had the day off. I was awakened suddenly by the loudest and most frightening noise I have ever heard in my life. It sounded as if the roof was being torn off the building. I was scared to death!

As I got up, I noticed several of the girls (nurses, physical therapists, dietitians) outside the barracks, looking up and very alarmed and frightened. We watched as the planes with orange circles (rising suns) flew low and recklessly over the hospital, turn around, and head back toward Wheeler Field (the fighter base about a quarter-mile away). We were completely amazed, confused, and afraid. The planes from Wheeler Field (fighter base) never flew directly over the hospital. These planes were so loud, so noisy and unfriendly, that we were petrified. We could all have been strafed or killed.

Within several minutes, the phone in quarters (our barracks) rang and we were advised that we were under alert. Then very shortly after, another call came telling us we were under "Red Alert," which meant "Report to duty station at once!"

Our instructions were, in case of emergency, all nonduty personnel should report to the "shack ward," which I did. As I entered the building, numerous stretchers were being brought in with wounded, bleeding soldiers from Wheeler Field. The Officer of the Day told us the wounded all needed operating room treatment immediately, but there was only one operating room and one operating team. He said, "All you can do is hold their hands and light their cigarettes."

I left the shack room as soon as sufficient nurses arrived. I am not a nurse and I couldn't give medication, but I did hold hands and light cigarettes, trying to bring comfort in any way I could.

All day and for several days, there was chaos, communication breakdowns, confusion, and rumors, but I have never witnessed the care and camaraderie that I saw during the day and the days following that I witnessed that time.

Dietary had little change in our routine of preparation of food, as all were too ill to eat or were dying. We stayed alert for information and instructions. We worked hard in getting our building bleached out. Rumors were flying fast and furious. Our greatest fear was the rumor that the Japanese were landing on the other side of the islands. This could not be confirmed or denied for many hours.

I received an honorable discharge in July 1945. My last duty station was Belvair, Virginia, as chief dietitian. My rank was first lieutenant, but today I would have been at least major or lieutenant colonel.

I am fully aware that this experience has made me realize how great it is to be an American and how proud I am of our armed forces, who keep us free, even under the dedication of their lives, so that all Americans can live in the greatest country in the world, as free people.

God bless America, and "Remember Pearl Harbor."

Pamela Waddell Bradbury, 1998

Lt. Harry C. Strawn in cockpit of British Spitfire MK-5, August 1942.

Harry Strawn

North African Theater, Army-Air Force
31st Fighter Group, 12th Air Force
413th Fighter Group, 14th Air Force

I was born in 1918 in Swissvale, Pennsylvania, a suburb of Pittsburgh. I graduated from the University of Pittsburgh in 1940 with a BA degree in business administration. After entering the Army Corps in 1941, I graduated on January 9, 1942, as a pilot.

During my service, I flew the O-52, P-39, P-40, British Spitfire, P-43, P-63, A-7, F-80, PT-19, BT-13, and the AT-6.

My combat time included the British Spitfire, MK-5, and the MK9, in England, North Africa, 125 hours combat, then in the Pacific, Okinawa, Japan, P47N, 145 hours.

I retired from the United States Air Force in 1970 as lieutenant colonel. I served in the Arkansas National Guard and several Air Force Reserve units for some thirty years. I now live in Springfield, Missouri, from November until May, then in Grand Lake, Colorado, from May to November.

In considering my experiences in World War II, there are many to choose from, but here are a few.

I was shot down twice in North Africa. The first time was by American ground troops and I was forced to crash-land my Spit 5 in the desert, shortly after a dogfight with a German 109 Messerschmitt. I made it back to my base, thanks to the help of an Army tank. My plane sustained 125 hits from light ground fire, none of which hit me.

After flying some 82 combat missions over North Africa, I

had a most remarkable experience. I had just received a new MK-9 Spitfire with new super-charged R. R. Merlin engine, and this gave me the ability to climb as fast as the German F. W. 190, and the ability to combat on even terms. This was not known by the German pilots, so we were able to surprise them for a few weeks. However, on this mission, I was flying at 30,000 feet with my squadron, when I spotted a German 190 below. I dove down after him. He saw me, I'm sure, and dove down to get away from me, but I was able to get close enough to squeeze off several bursts of fire and scored several hits on the FW-190. It began to smoke as I squeezed off the longer bursts with more hits.

However, I was now at a very low 8,000 or 10,000 feet, and my squadron was getting away from me. I began to climb back to join them at approximately 28,000 feet. I was hit by anti-air-craft, tearing off my right wing and setting my aircraft on fire. I knew I had to bail out, and not realizing I had taken a hit on my person, I began the sequence to bail out. When I released my

Harry Strawn, Mayor, Springfield, Missouri, Memorial Day, 1980.

safety harness, I tried to release the canopy, but my right fist was closed, so what action I took from there on was done with my left hand. (That is not natural.) Next, I stood up, preparing to jump, and when I did, my oxygen mask disconnected and I took two deep breaths and passed out.

The next thing I remember, I was looking at two German soldiers and they put me in their sidecar and took me to a German hospital in Tunis, Algeria. There, a fine German doctor operated on me, removing shrapnel from my right arm, shoulder, hip, and right leg. The operation took some seven hours, and I shall ever be grateful to this man. He relocated the ulnar nerve in my right arm, which allows me to have full use of my right arm (it hasn't helped my penmanship, though!).

After eight or nine weeks as a German prisoner, I was recaptured by the British army and returned to my unit (31st Fighter Group, 309th Squadron).

After several months in the British-American hospital recovering, I was assigned to the 413th Fighter Group. After several months training in P-47s, I went overseas to Okinawa, doing escort and fighter raids over Japan. I remained there until the Japs surrendered on Le Shima. This is just a taste of what the fighter pilots went through on a typical fighter mission.

Harold Edwards, 1940s.

Harold Edwards

U. S. Army
68th Battalion, 14th Regiment, Camp Fannin, Tyler Texas
81st Battalion, 15th Regiment, Company "B,"
Camp Fannin, Tyler, Texas
38th Division, Philippines
86th Blackhawk, 342nd Regiment, 3rd Battalion, Co. Headquarters
Discharge rank, Sergeant

I was born on March 19, 1925, in Omaha, Illinois, and started to school at the age of five. I loved school and had perfect attendance all twelve years, except for the days I missed when my mother died in 1931. I graduated in 1942 at the age of sixteen, and although the war had started, I was too young to be drafted, so I had to stay on the farm a few more years.

I was examined in October of 1944 in Chicago, Illinois, and after passing the examination was sent back home to wait. I was drafted on December 7, 1944, and at the age of eighteen was sent back to Chicago. I arrived at the South Street Station at 7:30 in the morning and was sworn in around 1:00 P.M. that afternoon. I was put in command of a group of five other boys. My job was to keep them on the train and keep them sober and calmed down. Why I was picked for this job, I don't know, unless the man who operated the draft board decided I was most qualified.

We were taken to Fort Sheridan, Illinois, to the barracks and had our picture made, which I still have to this day. We had a private that showed us around and started getting our issue. Our clothes were issued to us and we boxed up what we had on—our civilian clothes. They were mailed home. My father got upset when my clothes arrived and passed out. I didn't find this out until years later. I think he was sad to see me go.

It was my detail to fire the morning stove. I had never fired a coal stove, and it was a wonder I didn't burn the barracks down. When I was shipped out, they gave me a helmet with the "B" in it (which meant BINGO), plus your number. My number was B63, with an "A" which meant alternate. Then our numbers were called to board the train.

We left Illinois in a big snowstorm and arrived in East Texas at 11:00 at night at Camp Fannin in Tyler, Texas. Here I received six weeks of basic training and eight weeks of highly specialized training in Intelligence and Reconnaissance (I and R). This meant that I would obtain secret information and would pass it on to higher command. I was to question prisoners about troop movements and any weapons or equipment and was assigned to Company D, Battalion 68. The food was terrible, but it seemed simple. If you didn't want to eat it, you just left it on the tray. Little did I know that you eat it or else! After three attempts to discard the food, I devised a way to get out of the mess hall. I put it in my pocket and disposed of it somewhere else.

Before long, I was introduced to my new job, called KP, which is Kitchen Police. It was simple. You merely watch something like about fourteen hours of the cleaning of pots and pans, or various other chores. I'd get up about 4:00 A.M. to report to duty. At least you got your hands clean, or might I say red, because that soap would eat your hands up. Once my buddy Don Ely and I were on bivouac. It was late Sunday afternoon. We were itchy and antsy, so we were prowling around and came upon this bunker, and he thought it was an ammunition dump. We got to crawling around in there and discovered that it was a storage for food. We didn't get much milk to drink, not enough for me, anyway. I really liked milk, so we each drank a quart. The next morning in the chow line, one of the cooks was cussing, using words I had never heard of. He said that if he ever caught the two guys that drank his milk, well—. Little did he know that he was looking right at them. It wouldn't have been so funny if he hadn't made such a federal case out of it. To this day, every time my buddy and I get together, we always end up talking about the milk.

While in I and R, we trained with the .50-caliber machine gun, with mortar shells, and the bazooka—any type of destructive weapon. Then it came time for bivouac, which is out in the field training and is simulated battle conditions. This lasted two or three weeks.

I stayed in Texas until April 2, 1945, then was sent home on a ten-day furlough. My buddy Don Ely and I separated ways, not knowing if we would ever see each other again. Little did we know that in a few short days, we would be back together again. After my furlough, I took a train to Fort Ord, California, then boarded a ship.

On May 18, 1945, we landed at the Philippine Islands, where I was to stay for eighteen months. There I joined the 38th Division. We boarded a small landing craft, and got in the island of Luzon. The island was supposed to be secure—no more action. History has proven that to be a false statement. It was some of the bitterest, the bloodiest of the Japanese actions. They were in the hill part of the terrain. Inside there were rooms. The

Taken at the 59th Reunion of Camp Fannin. Left: Tommy Slaughter; right: Harold Edwards. The ladies are The Class Act *(a Dallas based dance group).*

Japanese used grenades and phosgene gas. The gas would burn you to pieces.

While in Luzon, I was assigned to take a briefcase of secret documents to Tacloban, Luzon. It involved the same airfield from which General MacArthur took off. A short time later, I was shipped back to Luzon, where I was present on July 4, 1946, when the Philippines won their independence. MacArthur was there for the celebration.

By the time we got to the 5th replacement depot, obviously, there were no lights. It had rained all day. That was the muddiest, slickest, sloppiest mud I had ever seen. The next day it was just beautiful. We all had to be processed again.

At the war's end, we stayed in Luzon approximately six more months, discharging Filipinos at the division headquarters. It was amazing how many prisoners we had taken, and how many were still left there. None were in good condition. Their clothes were tattered and worn, and they were hungry. We built stockades for them. If they had a problem, they took care of it themselves. They were behind protective fences, so I really never really developed a feeling for them. I had too many bitter memories of what their people had done.

From there we were sent to Manila to replace and train Filipino troops.

After arriving back in the States, we landed in Oakland, California, at an Army base. The first thing they did was give us all the milk we could drink. Except for that awful powdered milk, we had not had any fresh milk since we left.

Headed for home, I boarded a train. I didn't have my uniform on, for some reason. Some kids were just getting drafted and traveling on the train. A lady was talking to me about her son. Since I didn't have my uniform on, I had no stripes, no ID, no nothing. She thought I was some kind of upper-echelon commando. I woke up at Mount Carmi, Illinois and went into the restroom to change clothes. When I came out with my khakis, five ribbons, a Combat Infantry Badge, Overseas Badge, and buck sergeant stripes, the woman's eyes like to have fell out of her head. She had thought I was just on the street and had joined the service. She did show tears of joy.

It took nineteen days to arrive home by ship. I got $300

mustering-out pay, plus some travel pay I had coming. I got paid for furlough, which was a forty-five-day pay. The rank I had and the 20 percent overseas pay, plus the $10 CIB pay, all made a pretty good check.

When I got home, I had lost down to about 125 pounds and was very, very run down. I had malaria, which did not show up until the summer of 1947. I became very sick with the shakes and the sweats, which are the stinkingest mess. I had to take Atabrine. A side effect of Atabrine is that it will make your skin turn yellow. It will control the malaria as long as you take it, but when you quit taking it, the disease returns. Malaria is carried by the female mosquito. The disease will always be in my blood; it never goes away.

I wished many times that I had stayed on the train or simply gone back in the service. I went back to the farm and managed to make a living at it. In 1977, I had back surgery, in 1992 had a heart attack, then had a pacemaker put in in 1994.

After leaving the farm as a teenager, I had gone from a private on the front lines to a sergeant NCO, noncommissioned officer, in just five short months. It's been fifty-five years and the war seems like it was just yesterday.

Eldean Salmon

Army Air Corp, Pfc., 114th Infantry, Co I
384th Bomb Squadron Group H
544th Bomb Squadron, England

Eldean Salmon was born on March 25, 1921, in Elkhart, Texas. He was raised on a farm between Elkhart and Grapeland, Texas. Before entering the service, his occupation was that of a heat treater—a welder. He worked for Hughes Tool Company, Houston, Texas, as a welder. He entered the service on June 3, 1942.

He served in England, Northern France, Central Europe, and the Rhineland, with the 544th Bomb Squadron for a period of seventeen months. According to his separation papers form the Army of the United States, Eldean prepared food for Army personnel in the mess hall. He was familiar with government regulations governing kitchen sanitation. He prepared meats, soups, desserts, vegetables, and gravies in accordance with military standards and receipts.

He received an honorable discharge from the Army on October 20, 1945, at the Borden General Hospital, Chickasha, Oklahoma. Upon his discharge, he received the Distinguished Unit Badge, ETO Ribbon with three Bronze Stars, and the Good Conduct Medal.

On April 18, 1946, he entered the Air Force. His military occupation specialist was that of a welder combination. He completed the FEAF Consolidated School for Aircraft Welders. His military qualification were the Carbine MKM-152.

164

He received an honorable discharge from the Armed Forces of the United States on February 21, 1949, with the rank of staff sergeant, from the Air Force, having received the Victory Medal. He spent one year, ten months, and twelve days overseas.

Eldean Salmon's story was submitted by his son Barry. This is all that is known about his military service. Eldean died in 1990.

Eldean Salmon

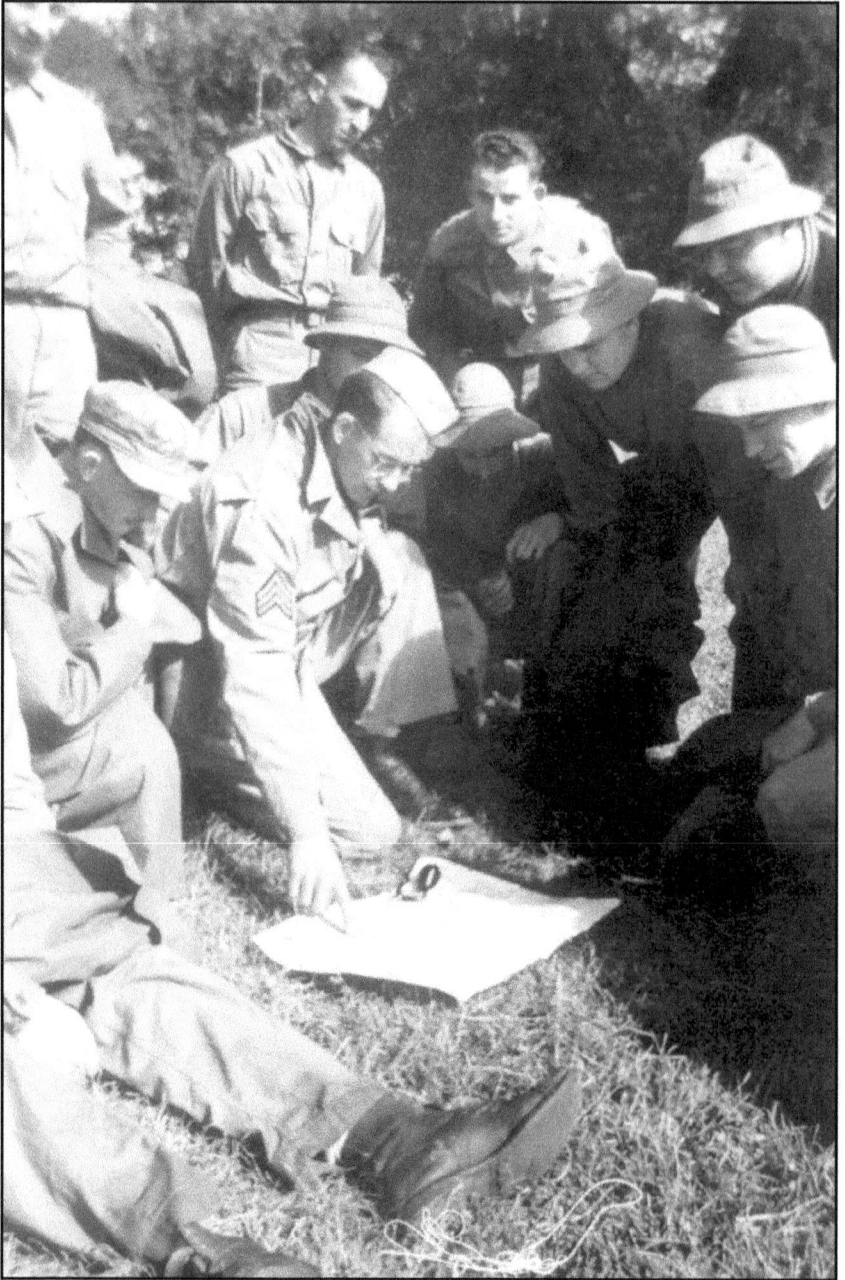

Howard Green (center, pointing) on a map-reading expedition in the 1940s.

Howard J. Green

6th Armored Division, 15th Tank Battalion
1875th Labor Supervision Company

I began my military service at Fort Dix, New Jersey, on August 21, 1941. I was then transferred to Fort Knox, Kentucky. After a short time there, I was sent to Gunnery Instructors School, where I graduated on February 7, 1942.

The winter at Fort Knox was a very cold one. We had small potbelly stoves that burned soft coal. The hard part was keeping the tents from catching fire, which they often did.

From Fort Knox, I was transferred to Camp Choffee, Arkansas, to be on the Cadre of the 6th Armored Division, teaching gunnery, map reading, and how to march. From there we went to Camp Cook, California, for desert maneuvers. The part I liked about being stationed in England was the catswalds, the small country towns. I can't remember the names of the towns we went through in France. I spent fifty-two days in the general hospital after receiving a bullet wound in the hip. Later I had to be hospitalized again because of the hip, but can't remember for how long. The Army nurses were wonderful, as were the ladies from the Red Cross.

I have forgotten many things that happened in my years of service, but one incident in particular I haven't forgotten. While in the hospital ward, a woman started singing. She was on a balcony above us and she had the voice of an angel. I have never heard anyone like her. The other patients tried to get her to sing more, but she disappeared as suddenly as she had come.

167

Mail was a big problem, especially if you moved around a lot, like going from the hospital to the replacement depot for re-assignment, then reporting to still another place.

My wife and I wrote each other most every day, whenever possible. I hadn't received mail for a long time on one occasion, when they came in and dumped a full mail sack onto my hospital bed. At another time, my wife baked some cookies for me and I received them a year to the day after she had mailed them. When I opened the package, I thought they were molded, but it was just the powdered sugar on them. They were delicious, "weren't they, guys?" We always shared. Since I received quite a few packages from home, my buddies always wanted to know where I was sleeping.

After being in two different hospitals in France, I was reassigned to the Army of Occupation, caring for German POWs. The POWs had their own kitchen. I have never tasted rye bread like they made. It was really good! They were quite a happy bunch, not having to fight anymore. Our company treated them well and they showed their appreciation. Most of them were not regular soldiers, much like ours. One was a master tailor, and he made a gown from a parachute for my wife. Another was an artist. He didn't have any materials or brushes to work with. He used whatever he would find. He painted a picture of my wife from a small picture I carried. His canvas was a piece of discarded barracks bag. It was perfect.

My wife kept a box of letters that I wrote to her, and last

Howard J. Green, 2000

year I read them. There is so much in them that I have no recollection of—friends that I knew or places where I was. I've tried to recall those times, but simply can't. One of them had a letter of recommendation from the Public Relations Office, and I can't remember any of it. According to my wife's records, I was promoted from staff sergeant to "Mister" (honorably discharged), on November 28, 1945.

My final word on war—WAR IS HELL!!!

Ira L. Simpson

566th Squadron, 389th Bomb Group

I was born on March 11, 1924, in Jackson, Mississippi. I graduated from Morton High School, Morton, Mississippi, in May 1941 and worked in private industry until entering military service.

In November of 1942, I enlisted in the Aviation Cadet Program and graduated from navigation training in March 1944. I was assigned to B-24 Aircraft in April 1943 at Westover Field, Massachusetts, where I met my crew. The pilot was Julius Weiss, the copilot Gerald Schaeffer, I was the navigator, the bombardier was Harold Heckler, the radio operator Clyde Hicks, engineer Robert Osbourne, tail gunner John Brown, nose gunner Carl Brewer, and two waist gunners Harry Jones and Alexander Kissmom. We received combat crew training at Charleston, South Carolina, April–June 1944, and Langley Field, Virginia, July 1944. The bombardier Heckler was taken off the crew at Langley for further training. The crew, without a bombardier, was transferred overseas in August 1944. The crew was assigned to the 566th Squadron, 389th Bomb Group, at Hethel, England, on September 2, 1944.

The officers were quartered in a concrete hut that housed two crews. There were nine men in the hut. We were given cots with British mattresses, which came in three sections and always separated during the night, making the bed very uncomfortable. We slept under two blankets most of the time because of

169

Ira L. Simpson, 1940s.

the cold temperature in England. The hut had a coal stove, and we were issued a small amount of coke each day to attempt to keep the hut warm. There was never enough coke to do this. The hut was always damp and cold. Each man had a rack on which to hang his clothes and a footlocker in which to keep other personal items.

The enlisted men of the crew were housed in a barracks with three other crews with about the same conditions as the officers. Our crew was in a Nissan hut rather than a concrete building.

The food was for the most part sufficient but not very appetizing, except on special occasions such as holidays and celebrations such as the 200th mission party. The mission party was a major event on the base. The bomb group did not fly that day. There were visiting dignitaries, and General Doolittle and General Spaatz reviewed the troops. After review, there was a special dinner and afterward a dance at the Officers and NCO clubs. Girls were brought in from the area around the base and from Norwich. Father Beck, the chaplain, kept a sharp eye on the festivities so there was not unseemly conduct.

Princesses Elizabeth and Margaret visited the group also. This was the only time that I saw any of the royal family. They toured the base and talked to some of the personnel and had lunch.

After additional flight training on Group and Eighth Air Force procedures, we flew our first combat mission, to Hamm, Germany, on October 2, 1944. There was quite a bit of anti-aircraft fire (flak) along the flight path. As we were a new crew, an experienced copilot flew with us instead of Gerald Schaeffer. Over the next several weeks, we flew across the Dutch coast north of Egmondann aan Zee; Kassel, Germany; East Anglia, Holland; Belgium; and eastern France.

In December 1944, we flew eight missions. On December 10, our target was Bingen, Germany, where we encountered heavy flak. One piece of flak cut my headphones off my helmet, but I was not injured. The pilot tried to contact me by intercom, but I did not hear him, as I was trying to put the earphone back on my helmet and had my helmet off. He thought I had been hit and sent the copilot down the nose to check on me. When the copilot found I was all right, he reported this to the crew. We lost one engine because of flak and could not stay in formation. Fortunately, we were not attacked by fighters, but we did receive some additional damage from ground fire. On December 19, our target was the railroad yards at Ehrand, Germany. This was the first raid in support of the efforts to contain the German advance during the Battle of the Bulge.

The weather prevented future attacks until December 24, when the weather over Belgium and Germany cleared enough to allow us to bomb. During this time, we would be briefed on a mission and go tour aircraft and stand by all day waiting for the weather to clear over the target area. The weather in England was very bad, and we had to take off in fog and rain and climb up to above 7,000 feet before we got above the clouds. Several aircraft crashed on takeoff, and we could see the plumes of smoke rising through the clouds.

On our second mission to Koblenz, we received extensive damage to our aircraft but did not have any crew members injured. Our next mission was to Bonn, on January 6, 1945, to bomb the railroad bridge across the Rhine River. We encountered moderate flak and had damage to one engine. Again we were unable to keep up with the formation and had to return to the base alone. Flying this number of missions in a very short time made us extremely tired. Even on the days we did not fly, we would be on standby and had to get up at 4:30 or 5:00 A.M. for briefing and stay on alert most of the day.

On January 16, our target was the oil refinery at Madgeberg, Germany. We received moderate damage to our aircraft and had to leave formation. The weather became very bad, and because of damage and the loss of fuel, we diverted to northern France. After searching for an airfield for about thirty minutes, we saw a break in the clouds and spotted a former German fighter airfield, located near Denain, France. Before we could make an approach for landing, the weather closed in and we were again flying on instruments. The pilot made a turn to the right and made a circle to align the plane with the runway. We began a descent to the field, but when we broke out of the overcast, we were about 45 degrees to the runway and had to try again.

After two more tries, we managed to land. As the aircraft

touched down, we saw a B-17 on the runway. It had crashed on landing. The pilot had to brake hard and turn the aircraft to the side to avoid a collision. The runway was very short, but we managed to stop just short of hitting the other plane. Due to the damage to our plane and the short length of the runway, the plane was left behind on the airfield. The bombsight was removed from the aircraft, and after contact was made with American Army personnel in the area, we went into the town of Valenciennes and found a motel for the night.

Shortly after returning to base, one of our gunners, Alexander Kissimom, fell off a bicycle and broke his ankle. Therefore he was unable to fly. Also, on February 3, another gunner, Carl Brewer, flew with another crew and was shot down. The plane exploded, and Carl was killed. This made all the crew very sad, and our morale was quite low.

Our crew didn't fly a combat mission again until February 14. Our target was Madgeberg again. There were no enemy fighters along our flight until we got near Madgeberg. The American fighters drove them off without any losses. Over the target, we received major damage to the area in the forward part of the bomb bay, just after we dropped our bombs. Our fuel transfer system was knocked out, and we were unable to transfer fuel, which became very important later. Also, one engine was severely damaged and set on fire. The fire was extinguished, but the engine was inoperable and we were unable to feather the propeller. Feathering the propeller meant turning the propeller blade to a position where it did not cause any drag on the aircraft because of air resistance. This later caused a problem in maintaining air speed when we lost power on a second engine. Again we had to drop out of formation.

The controls were damaged, but Osborne, the engineer, managed by various methods and all his tools—a pair of pliers and a couple of screwdrivers to patch them up enough to keep us in the air. Afterward, the tail turret was blasted nearly off, throwing the tail gunner, Harry Jones, back into the waist. Next, the top turret was knocked out by flak. Up in the nose, John Brown was standing outside his turret with his chute on, ready to bail out or to get into his turret in the event of fighters.

The pilot asked for assistance, and a P51 aircraft came and

flew off our wing until we were almost out of Germany, when we had to return to base because we were low on fuel. During this time, we lost the second engine and could not maintain flying speed of more then 100 knots. This made the plane stall occasionally and lose altitude. Losing altitude and over an undercast, we made our way back to Holland. The plane was just mushing through the air, keeping a little above stalling speed by pulling all the power possible on the three engines that were left.

As we crossed the Zuider Zee, a boat picked us up and began firing. The shots nearly all went wild, but a few passed through the ship, frightening us again. We were shot down to 4,000 feet when we crossed over the Dutch coast and the North Sea.

When we reached the North Sea, we turned toward Belgium and flew down the coast of Holland. There we were picked up again by shore batteries, which were fairly accurate and shot us up very badly. Finally, another engine started sputtering for lack of fuel. We couldn't get the 150 gallons in the tank of the engine that was out, because the fuel transfer system was damaged. Therefore, the pilot, Julius Weiss, turned over in over land and gave the order to bail out.

Before bailing out, I had gone up on the flight deck from the nose, after a 20mm had gone through the nose. As the order was given to bail out, I checked my chute and found it was on backward, so I changed it quickly. The engineer, Ozzie, and the radio operator, Clyde Hicks, went out and I then followed them out through the bomb bay.

The slipstream grasped me as soon as I was outside the plane and whisked me away from the plane. There was the most pleasant sensation of just riding on air and not falling. It was not at all as I had imagined it would be. I immediately pulled my chute, for I was only about 2,000 feet when I left the ship. The chute opened very quickly without any trouble. I saw I was approaching some high-powered electric lines, so I tried to slip my chute to avoid hitting them. When I did this, I caused my chute to partially collapse, making my descent faster than normal. I landed in an apple orchard behind a farmer's house and struck the ground very hard, knocking myself unconscious.

Upon regaining consciousness, I found myself surrounded by Dutch people and a German coming up to me. I struggled up to my feet and found that the Dutch farmer's wife had removed my chute and my Mae West, or life preserver. The Germans immediately took my pistol and put me in a wagon. I was taken over to where my tail gunner, John Brown, lay and found he had been killed when he bailed out. The body was put on the wagon, and we were taken to a small encampment. I was searched and all my personal things were removed, along with my escape kit and maps. The German officer told me that Brown would be buried in a local cemetery.

Later I was taken to a bunker where I joined George Lozier, the left waist gunner, but we were separated for the night. I spent the night alone, in a room above the headquarters, wondering what was going to happen to me and about where the rest of the crew was and if they had survived.

The next morning, George and I were taken through Oostvoorne to where the rest of the crew was being held. Although I was in pain from the blow to my head when I had landed, and my vision was blurred, I felt better when I saw that everyone was safe. I never did receive any medical treatment for the head injury or the minor wound on my leg. All of us were taken by truck to a prison in Rotterdam. We spent the next three nights there. We then moved to a German base at Amsterdam, where the copilot and I were separated from the rest of the crew.

After a brief interrogation, we learned we were to be moved into Germany, with the pilot going to the hospital, as he had broken his ankle when he bailed out. I never saw him again. The co-pilot and I traveled to Frankfurt, along with four other officers from other planes that had been shot down. The first night out, we passed through Dortmund, which had just been bombed by the British. It was quite a sight to behold. We had to leave the train on one side of the town and walk through to a train station on the other side. There were fires all around us and delayed action bombs still going off. We were very apprehensive and were wondering if we would be able to get through the city.

We made it okay, but when we got to the train station and were waiting for the train, some of the civilians became very angry and began to threaten us, saying we were the gangsters who bombed women and children. The situation became very tense, and we did not know if we were going to get out of there alive. The guards moved us away from the crowd, but they followed making threatening gestures and calling the guards protectors of criminals. The guards pointed their guns at the crowd and made them stay away. A train came shortly afterward and the guards rushed us to the train and into a compartment and secured the doors. After another day, we arrived at the interrogation center in Frankfurt on February 19.

The first two days I spent in solitary confinement without seeing anyone except the guards, when they fed me breakfast and at noon and night. Our meals consisted of two slices of bread and a little jam for breakfast, thin, watery soup at noon (about a pint), and another sandwich at night. Therefore, we were always hungry. We had no cigarettes, which we really missed. There were no books or any way of entertaining our minds except to lie on the bed and think about what had happened and about what would happen to us next. The bed was wooden, with one blanket, which did not keep out the cold. My room had a window, which I managed to open and could look out when the guards weren't around.

The third day, in the afternoon, I was taken to an office for interrogation. After the interrogation, a German major found I wasn't answering his questions, so he began telling me things about my outfit, which I thought were secret. After about three hours of discussion, he told me I could go back to my room and could get a shave and a bath, and that I would leave the next afternoon.

The next morning, I got the shave and bath. I spent the day reading a book given to me by the guard. It was written in English but was about Germany. About 5:00, the guards came and told me I was leaving, so I went outside and fell in with the other men that were being sent to the prison camp.

That night we were taken to the station and put on a train for Wetzlar. We traveled all night and all the next day, until 2:00 in the morning. We arrived at Wetzlar Sunday morning, February 26, 1945. We had to wait until 8:00 for the Germans to come and search us and to fill out some forms for the Red Cross. They also fingerprinted us. Afterward, we were taken across the road and into the camp, where we were given a shower. We were each issued a Red Cross kit with soap, shaving soap, and cigarettes. We were issued underwear, shoes, and a very welcome overcoat. There were also a few other items, such as a razor, razor blades, and tooth powder.

We were then given a good hot meal, our first meal in Germany. It was also our last, until we were liberated. I then met my enlisted men again and went to church with them. Later in the day, I met William Rogers, a boy I went to high school with. We were not allowed to talk long, as the guards made us separate. After spending the night and part of the next day at the camp, we were shipped out to the prison camp at Nuremberg.

After a five-day ride on the train, which ordinarily took about four hours, we arrived at our destination. It was very cold and snowing at Nuremberg. Nearly everyone froze their feet, because we had to stand in snow for about half a day while we went through the old routine of forms and fingerprinting. Later in the afternoon, we were assigned our barracks and managed to get a little warmth from three small fires. This was March 4, 1945. There were sixteen men in our room in the barracks, including two Tuskegee pilots. Another man was from New York. He entertained us sometimes with stories of Brooklyn.

The first two weeks were miserable and horribly cold. We had to live on a seventh of a loaf of bread and about half a pint of thin soup, usually made from potato peels or rutabagas. Sometimes the potato peels were rotten. We were given some hot water in the morning, the bread at noon, and the soup at night. The black bread was made with sawdust as a filler and was very sour-tasting. We ate it, nevertheless. During all the time I was in prison camp, I was hungry and cold. The main topic of conversation among the men was food. We would make up recipes for food that we were going to cook when we got back to the United States.

After about two weeks, we received another shower and our first Red Cross parcel, which was very welcome. It contained a can of Spam, a can of stew, five packages of cigarettes, prunes, jam, coffee, a can of liver pâté, a can of margarine, and a tin of twelve crackers. This, in addition to our German rations, had to last us a week. Afterward, we received the parcels at irregular intervals.

On March 29, the Germans brought thirty-two Serbian

generals into our compound, and it was very interesting to speak with them, as some could speak a little English. The Germans later executed these men, before the Americans arrived.

At last the day came we had all dreaded. We were to move to Moosberg, about 160 kilometers, or 100 miles, away. Everything was in an uproar all morning until at 1:30 P.M. on April 2, we moved out of camp. We marched in columns of three or four and by compounds. After we left camp, we marched east of the town of Feucht and south to the town of Neumarkt. In late afternoon it began to rain and continued throughout the night. We were not allowed to stop except for short breaks of fifteen minutes up until 3:00 A.M. At that time we stopped at a lumber mill, and some of us could get out of the rain under a shed. We tried to sleep, but the cold and rain made that almost impossible. At dawn the rain had stopped and we resumed the march. At about 10:00 A.M. we reached Neumarkt and stopped. We were told that we would be given soup later. Shortly after noon, the guards brought a large kettle of soup to us and we all received a bowl of it. It was potato soup, I believe. This was the first food we had received since the morning before. About this time, the 8th Air Force bombers flew overhead toward Nuremberg. We all watched as they opened their bomb bay doors for the bomb run.

About 2:00 A.M. our column was ordered to march through the town and continue south toward Berching. The weather was sunny but still cold, so we were glad to get moving. After walking for about four hours, we came to a village where we were put in the farmers' barns for the night. There was one guard assigned to each barn.

The next morning about 7:00 A.M. we were ordered to continue and marched all day with only short breaks. We arrived at Berching in the afternoon and received a Red Cross food parcel. We traded cigarettes to the farmers for potatoes. Therefore, we had a good meal that night. The next day, we were strafed by two P-47s as we walked alongside a railroad through a small village. I crawled under a pile of lumber nearby until the planes left. We were told that some people were hurt and two killed. After this occurrence, some signs were made indicating that we were POWs. Two days later, we saw several P-38 aircraft that flew over the column and indicated they knew who we were. After that, almost every day we would see fighters scouting out positions. I am sure they were reporting the progress of the march.

It began raining again, and we were all stiff and wet. Again the Germans made us march at night. I became quite ill but was not allowed to stop and rest. About 10:00 P.M., we came to a village and we were allowed to sleep in the church. We were wet, cold, and hungry, and had nothing to eat.

The next day, the weather was better and we dried out and were not so cold. I was still ill, but one of the other prisoners helped me by carrying my pack. We did not march far that day and stayed in a barn that night. We found a milk can on the road that had milk in it, so we drank it. The next morning, I traded cigarettes for some eggs, which the farmer's wife cooked for me. Most of the farmers were not hostile and would trade with us for food.

By the next morning, I had recovered from my illness, so I was able to continue. We moved about six kilometers to a village of Sanderdorf, where we stayed for three days. Everyone was exhausted, and all we did was sleep and rest. We received part of a Red Cross food parcel while we were there.

On April 13, we learned that President Roosevelt had died and were very sad. There was a brief ceremony and prayer led by one of the officers.

We arrived in Mooseberg on April 15, and I was assigned a barracks near the end of the camp. Living conditions were worse than in Nürnberg. We were very crowded and had little space to move about. The three-tiered bunks were only about twelve inches apart. We did have running water in the ward, so were able to wash and shave. We were issued two Red Cross parcels before the Americans liberated us on April 29, so we did have some food.

On the morning of the 29th, when we went outside the barracks, the guards were gone, so we knew something was happening. About 10:00 A.M., we heard firing and tanks. Some of the bullets were coming into camp, so we were told to stay inside. However, we were curious about what was happening, so we would occasionally go outside. The battle was between the Americans and German SS troops. We heard later that the SS troops were there to execute all the prisoners in compliance with

Hitler's orders that all POWs be killed. Near noon, an American tank came into camp. All the American prisoners swamped it. At 12:35 P.M., the American flag was raised over the camp and Americans took control. I don't believe there was a dry eye among us as we watched our flag go up.

There was a lot of celebrating that day and night. The next day, General Patton came into camp and talked with us. He instructed his aides to make arrangements for us to get food and said that we should be going home soon. We were asked to remain in camp until arrangements could be made to get us out. However, many of the POWs left camp to try to rejoin their units or get transportation back to the United States. The majority stayed in camp.

On May 5, the men from my barracks were taken by truck to an airfield at Landshut for air transportation to Camp Lucky Strike at Fecamp, France.

There was a delay, as there were not enough aircraft to fly all of us out that day. I went with one of the truck drivers into town, and we drove around sightseeing. We went into several houses, but there was no one in them. After about an hour, we heard shooting and realized that there were still German snipers around, so we drove back to the airfield.

Later that day, shortly after noon, a German aircraft buzzed the field and all of us hit the ground, as we thought that we could see bombs under the wing. The infantrymen guarding the airfield began shooting at the plane but fortunately did not hit it. The pilot landed and came out of the plane with his hands up. He had his wife and children with him. They were taken away by the troops.

The next day, May 6, 1945, we were loaded in C-47 aircraft and flown to Rheims, France, and taken to a processing center where we received new uniforms, got a hot shower and shave, and were fed our first hot meal since the one at the interrogation center. The next morning we learned that the Germans had signed the Surrender Documents at General Eisenhower's headquarters that night. We left Rheims, flew to LeHarve, and were taken by trucks back to Camp Lucky Strike. The French people were celebrating, and as our trucks drove through the village, they would throw flowers at us. They also gave us wine and cheese. If we stopped, they would climb aboard and shake our hands.

At Camp Lucky Strike, I saw our flight engineer. He said that all the men were okay, but had been separated. After about two weeks I was sent to a camp at LeHarve to wait for a ship to return to the States. On June 12, we arrived in New York. Once at Camp Shanks, New York, we were told the mess hall would be open twenty-four hours a day and we could order anything we wanted. Normally, we had to eat what the cooks prepared or not at all. Most of us ordered steaks, French fries, milk, and ice cream. Some of the men ate too much and were sick. Our stomachs had shrunk when we were in prison camp because we did not get enough food. Our systems could not tolerate rich foods.

Ira L. Simpson, 2000

The next day we left on a train for Camp Shelby, Mississippi. The trip took three days. Once there, we were given sixty days' leave, after which I was to report to Miami Beach for further processing and return to duty.

Raymond "Hap" Halloran

Raymond "Hap" Halloran

B-29 Bomber Training, Salina, Kansas,
878th Squadron, 499th Bomb Group
V.H. 73rd Wing, 20th Air Force-
B-29 Bomber Crew, "Rover Boys Express"
POW-Survivor

I was born in Cincinnati (Lockland), Ohio, on February 4, 1922. Early in 1942, I volunteered for the Army Air Corps, at Wright Field, Dayton, Ohio. I completed training as a navigator in Hondo, Texas, in 1943 and completed training as a bombardier in Roswell, New Mexico, in 1944. Later I was assigned to B-29 Bomber Training at Smokey Hill Air Force Base, Salina, Kansas, 878th Squadron, 499th Bomb Group V. H. 73rd Wing, 20th Air Force.

After completion of B-29 training, I and my crew of eleven men from eleven different states, called "Rover Boys Express," spent time in Lincoln, Nebraska, then in Herrington, Kansas, where we received our own B-29. Orders were to fly our new B-29 across the Pacific alone to John Rogers Field, Hawaii, then to Kwajalein Island. From there we went to Saipan, an 8,000-mile flight which we flew alone, where the 73rd Wing Base was located. Saipan was an island in the Marianas, recently secured by the Marines, Army, and Navy. We were to fly combat missions to bomb and destroy Japanese mainland targets.

We flew missions to Iwo Jima, Nagoya, Kobe/Akashi in December 1944 and January 1945, before we were shot down on the fourth mission—target #357 Nakajima Aircraft Factory,

Tokyo. We were eastbound at 32,000 feet, passing Mt. Fuji when we were shot down over Tokyo by a Japanese Twin Engine Toryu (Nick) Fighter that came in from ten o'clock high. Three engines were on fire. We had to parachute into Tokyo when the fighter blew out the nose; the 70-plus-degree temperature in our pressurized B-29 dropped instantly to -58 degrees below zero.

I fell free from 27,000 feet to approximately 3,000 feet before opening my chute and landing in northeastern Tokyo. With my face and hands frozen from the high-altitude bailout, I was set upon immediately by about 1,000 civilians, and severe beatings followed. I was hit with sticks, punched, kicked, and stoned, and was near death when Japanese soldiers (MPs from Kempei Tai Secret Service Torture Prison) seized me from the civilians. They cut up my chute, tied my hands to my ankles, and tossed me in the back of a truck to be taken to Kempei Tai Torture Main Prison in Tokyo, adjacent the moat at the north edge of the Imperial Palace grounds.

For six days, I was in a four-by-five-foot cell with two Japanese criminals. I was interrogated, beaten, starved, threatened with death, and was the target of other horrible treatment. I was then dragged across the snow to a stable where I spent sixty-seven days in solitary confinement in a cold, dark horse stall. Beatings and brutal interrogations continued. I had very little to eat, usually rice about the size of a golf ball for a meal.

I lived through the March 10, 1945, fire raid on Tokyo where over 100,000 were killed by B-29s bombing from 0100 to 0400 hours. The heat, smoke, and firestorms were absolutely terrifying.

Then I was moved to Ueno Zoo in Tokyo, where I was a prisoner in an animal cage and tied to the front bars in a lion cage, so civilians could march by and view a B-29 flyer, the reason being to humiliate me and show the Japanese that the B-29 crews weren't supermen. I was naked and black from being unwashed, and I had hair all over my face. I had lost ninety pounds and was covered with open, running sores from flea and bedbug bites.

I spent from April 1, 1945, to August 1945, in Omori POW camp contiguous southwestern Tokyo. Along with B-29 crew members plus several Navy and Marine flyers, I was placed in a "special barracks" reserved for the select group who had been forced to sign a statement (in Japanese) acknowledging that we had indiscriminately bombed and killed Japanese civilians. Thus we were not POWs but federal prisoners on trial for our lives. They also waived Geneva Convention rules governing POW treatment. Beatings and torture, malnutrition, no letters in or out, no Red Cross packages (guards took them), no soap, no baths. Such was life in Tokyo.

Gregory "Pappy" Boyington, who was to become a lifelong a friend, was also in my barracks. He was a member of the Blacksheep Squadron and after having been shot down was picked up by a Japanese submarine and taken to Rabaul. He was eventually taken to Omori POW camp. This began a friendship which lasted forty-three years, until Pappy died in 1988 of cancer. He was a real Marine hero and the original "Top Gun" holder of the Congressional Medal of Honor. I delivered the eulogy at Pappy's funeral, which was held in the Arlington National Cemetery.

On August 29, 1945, we were liberated by Marine/Navy landing forces and taken aboard the hospital ship *Benevolence* in Tokyo Bay. I spent about a year in Ashford General Hospital, in White Sulpher Springs, West Virginia. I was honorably discharged from the service in September of 1946 and was near the Battleship *Missouri* when the Peace Treaty was signed on September 2, 1945.

I have experienced thirty-nine years of nightmares after that ordeal. Later I returned to Tokyo in 1984–85, 1989, and 1995, where I met Ambassador Mike Mansfield, who was a great help. I was also reunited with a former guard (friendly) and many others, including: Kaneyuki Kobayashi, former guard; Saburo Sakai, leading living Japanese fighter ace (now friend); and Isamu Kashiide, who shot down our B-29 over Tokyo on January 27, 1945. Reconciliation and friendships finally eradicated the nightmares of thirty-nine years.

In 1998, I wrote a book called *Hap's War*, which is the incredible survival story of a POW slated for execution. Today, my philosophy is "With God's help adversity makes you a stronger person. Forget about animosity, enjoy life! Enjoy freedom! Put everything into life for your fellowman."

Sgt. Jim S. Burleson, age eighteen, October 1943, Pecos (Pyote), Texas, air base.

Jim S. Burleson

United States Army Air Corps
91st Bomb Group (H)
401 Squadron S/Sgt
POW Stalag 17-B Kerms, Austria

I was born in Houston, Texas, on December 15, 1924. I enlisted at the age of eighteen in November 6, 1942, and was discharged just before age twenty-one, on November 2, 1945. As part of the Campaign-Air Offensive in Europe, I was shot down on my eighth mission over Cherbourg, France, on April 27, 1944. At the age of nineteen, my rank was staff sergeant for the 91st Bomb Group 401 Squadron. Our B-17 Fortress, named *Mary* by our pilot for his wife, had completed nine missions before this run.

Just before the target over the French coast, a V-weapon launch site, we were hit in the nose under the instrument panel. The plane went into a spin, pinning us all to the floor. The autopilot was switched on, and it was able to pull the plane out of the spin for a short time. We began to bail out. The tail gunner went through three spins before getting out. Eyewitnesses reported seeing the ship leaving the formation, apparently out of control, with a stream of smoke pouring from the No. 3 engine.

Only five chutes were counted before the plane hit the ground and exploded in a fireball, but nine of the crew actually survived. I bailed out of the spinning plane at about 18,000 feet and made a delayed opening, my chute barely opening before hitting the ground.

The Germans were waiting for us on the ground. I was waist gunner, and my ball turret gunner, landed in the next pasture from me. The Germans put us in a truck and we were driven to the crash site. At the site, we were shown the body of our dead radio operator. Otto Mathis, the navigator, received a compound fracture to his leg from flak fragments and was hospitalized, but the rest of the crew were sent for interrogation. I remember being held under guard in a cell in Paris. That was quite an experience, seven of us wedged in one cell, listening to the yells and screams throughout the night. I was glad we were together rather than alone.

The crew were finally taken to Dulag Luft. Later, noncoms were sent on boxcars, which took five days and nights, to Stalag 17B, a Nazi prison camp located in Keerms, Austria, about thirty miles east of Vienna.

Jim Burleson, 2000

In April 1945 we were forced to march for twenty-one days from Kerms, Austria, about 280 miles to lower Braunau, Hitler's birthplace. We were held in a barbed-wire compound in the forest near there. We received Red Cross parcels occasionally, which we usually shared with two or more other men. The Germans fed us hot water sawdust bread and a couple of small potatoes, and some kind of soup, most of the time.

One side of the camp was composed of about 4,000 of us, and the other side held about the same amount of Russian, French, Serbian, and Italian prisoners. As airmen, we did not work, but the other side of the camp did. We were able to trade cigarettes for some things they were able to get while working on the farms etc.

The Red Cross and YMCA were able to send books and other items to occupy our time. The camp was overcrowded and the barracks were without heat. After the twenty-one-day forced march, we were put into a wooded area without shelter for several days, sleeping on the ground. Some of the men made lean-tos for shelter. It rained, snowed, and was cold. After several days of this, Patton's Third Army came across the river and liberated us. We had to wait two days before we could be transported back to our lines.

Olney N. Nygaard

11th Regiment, 54th Battalion, Company C
U.S. Army, Camp Fannin, Texas
4th Field Artillery, 68th Medical Depot (End of War)

Story One

During World War II in basic training, we had just finished an obstacle course and were standing in ranks at attention. Unbeknownst to me, my bayonet had become dislodged from my field pack and was obviously missing.

When the company commander was conducting inspection, he asked me the question, "Private, where is your bayonet?" I had no recourse but to say, "I do not know, sir."

He snapped, "Well, Private, you had better shit one!" My reply was, "I will try, sir."

No challenge in my life has ever equaled that one.

Story Two

Our last excursion was down the road of factual ridiculousness. Shall we now take a short stroll down the path of semi-silliness?

Our training cycles at Camp Fannin ended July 10, 1945, after which we were granted a few days' leave of absence before reporting to Fort Ord, California.

It was during our leave (July 16) that the successful testing

190

Olney N. Nygaard, 1940s.

of the atomic bomb had occurred in the New Mexico desert. (This of course, we later learned.) While I was at Fort Ord, both atomic bombs were dropped on Japan, on August 6 and August 9. Five days later, August 14, Japan agreed to surrender.

We were then sent to March Field in southern California. After a few days there, on August 20, we boarded a banana boat, the *Cape Neddick,* which had been converted into a troop ship. We could never forget as we boarded, the playing by the Army Band of the popular song of that time, "Sentimental Journey."

On September 2, V-J day, we were somewhere between Pearl Harbor and the Marshall Islands. After a short stay at Eniwetok (Marshall Islands), we set sail for the Philippine Islands.

Although the Americans had gained control of the Philippines as a result of the Spanish-American War half a century before, elements of Spanish culture could easily be detected. On the island of Luzon, on which the city of Manila is located, there was a language dialect that the Filipinos spoke, called Tagalog.

But the Filipinos' pronunciation of English words was almost identical to that of our Spanish-speaking friends, even here in Texas. (i.e., short vowel "i" in English pronunciation = long vowel "e" in Spanish pronunciation). You can imagine the mixed emotions I had when the Filipino gals would gaze at me and exclaim, "Looks like a weener!" (winner).

I am sure that it was at Camp Fannin that we were told of the comparison of armies of two different eras of the century. Soldiers of World War II = Singing Army, and the soldiers of World War II were the "wise-cracking" Army.

P.S. Upon reviewing this story, it seems to be more fact than fiction.

Story 3
National Patriotism

The following is simply an amusing story that I have heard for forty or fifty years and decided to write it up for part of my story. I don't know who originally came up with it.

Although war clouds were beginning to form in the 1930s,

there was a great division in the public sentiment on the debate as to the question of which direction or role the United States should play in the upcoming world turmoil.

Those who supported the policies of isolationism and pacifism prevented the United States from supporting England in the manner that Prime Minister Churchill requested and pleaded.

Because of Japan's ruthless treatment of China, the United States placed an oil embargo on Japan in the summer of 1941. At that time, Japan had enough oil to supply their military for only six months. There was plenty of oil in Singapore and other places in the Far East. But Japan's access to that oil was blocked by the presence of the United States Navy in the Pacific.

When negotiations between Japanese ambassadors and the United States failed to drop the oil embargo, Japan set in motion their already planned naval and air attack on Pearl Harbor and other military instillations in Hawaii. The following day, the United States Congress declared war on Japan and a couple of days later, on Germany.

Sentiments of isolationism and pacifism virtually disappeared, and the country was united in a spirit of patriotism to a measure that some historians and scholars doubt could ever be repeated.

And then there was this "wise-crack" story about the war bonds drives. These drives were so successful that it was brought to the attention of bureaucrats in Washington that war bonds had been purchased in every place in the country with the exception of one town in the Ozark Mountains. A decision was made to send an investigator to explore the possibility of un-American activities or feelings there. As the investigator drove into the town, he stopped to talk with a group of men gathered at the town square. When he posed questions to them about the war bonds drive, he immediately began to sense the town's insulation from the rest of the world, a trait for which the Ozarks had a notable reputation.

The investigator questioned the townsmen:

Investigator: "You must be familiar with the name Franklin Roosevelt?"

Townsmen: "No, we don't know him."

Investigator: "Well, you must have heard of Pearl Harbor?"

Townsmen: "No, we don't know her either."

Having all the information he needed, the investigator headed back to Washington. Another townsman came up and asked the group, "What did the man in the new car want?" One of them answered, "We don't know exactly, but it was something about a Mr. Franklin Roosevelt getting into trouble with Miss Pearl Harbor and he wanted us to go his bond."

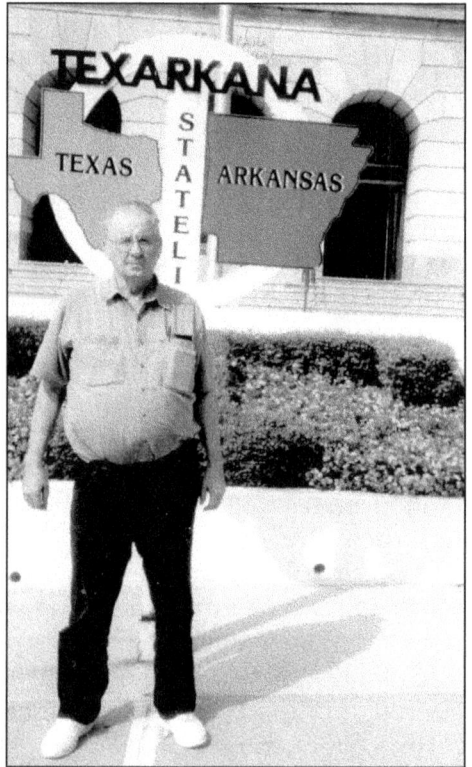

Olney N. Nygaard, 2000

Norman Kellman

79th Infantry Division, Company E
9th Army at war's end

This is a lengthy, two-part letter that Norman wrote home to his wife, a documentary of his tour in the European theater, mainly in France.

Germany, May 15, 1945

Dearest Betty,

Hello, Honey. I just found out that quite a few restrictions have been lifted as to censorship, so I'm going to let go with the works as much as I can remember. Of course, I can't mention where I am now, but I can tell you some of the towns we fought for back in the region of Alsace in Northeastern France.

As you know, I left the States October 22, 1944. As far as the trip was concerned, it was uneventful. We had "abandoned ship" and alert drills about every other day.

On the twelfth day, we sighted the southernmost tip of England. The next day we docked at Southampton, but only to go from one ship to another. So in other words, I had been on English soil for about ten minutes.

We left that evening and anchored in the English Channel for the night. The next morning we traveled down towards Cherbourg, France, and stopped off at Omaha Beach. Omaha Beach is where the initial invasion landing was made on June 6,

Norman Kellman, S/Sgt., Company E.

1944. A large landing craft, I believe it was an LCT, came up to the boat and we loaded up on it. The surrounding water was littered with all sorts of debris and wrecked ships. The beach was torn up but traffic moved around pretty smoothly. About 800 yards across the beach was the base of a large hill. I thought I would nearly pass out halfway up with all the stuff I was carrying.

We had to walk about three miles to where we were to stay. This place turned out to be a space surrounded by hedgerows. We pitched tents there that night. The weather at that time was very damp and rainy. There was quite a lot of mud just to make things more enjoyable.

We spent about two or three days there just laying around waiting for transportation. Finally, some trucks came and we loaded up and traveled to a place about six or seven miles from LeMans. Again we pitched tents and waited.

After several more days, we packed up and hiked about five miles with a full load to a railroad station. There we loaded up and traveled for three days and two nights over what seemed to be all of France.

We finally ended up at Thaon-les-Vosges, which is near Epinal, just west of Alsace. There they sorted out the men to the various divisions. After five days, we were issued weapons and moved again to Luneville.

Luneville was where everyone got his final check. This is also the place where Harry and I got "stinko" on champagne. Finally we were given a lecture on where we were heading and what to expect.

We loaded on trucks and were on our way. All along the way were various forms of destruction but here it looked more recent. In the distance we could hear the deep rumbling become louder and louder.

Night was approaching as we passed the first batteries of artillery pieces. They were the long distance 155mm "Long Toms." We traveled to a town where we finally unloaded and were taken to our individual companies. From there we were platooned and then directed to individual squads. It was too dark at the time to actually get acquainted with anyone right away. We were too tired anyway, from the long trip. Our squad spent the night in a hay-loft. I didn't sleep well that night because the artillery made so much noise and besides I was nervous.

The next day we were up at 6 A.M. and ate our K rations "Breakfast Unit." Our company had been moved to the rear in reserve before I arrived, so we were a couple of towns in back of the front lines. We waited around until we got orders to move up to the next town.

We moved out and it was on this trip that I experienced my first bit of artillery when a couple of German shells landed about 500 yards from the road we were on. This started my ol' heart a pumping. I sure was scared.

We got to the next town and settled down in a barn for a rest. Later on we moved to a nearby school building where there was more room. About 8 that evening, the Germans started to shell the town heavily. They kept it up almost all night. We would have moved to the basement, but it was full of civilians. I didn't get any sleep that night, I was so scared!

About five in the morning, our platoon leader came in and told us that we were going to attack the next town. You can imagine how I felt after hearing that! We went through the process of mapping out our plans. Then at seven, we pushed off.

We had several tanks to support us in our advance. There was a large open field that we had to cross before we could reach the town. Our artillery threw in smoke shells which screened our movement, but the Germans must have had some observation on us because as soon as we got out in the open, they started to shell us. I wasn't exactly what you would called scared but I know that my heart was racing like hell! I wasn't used to the sound of various kinds of shells or how close they would come, so every time I heard one coming, I hit the dirt. Some of them landed a half mile away and yet I hit the dirt. I wasn't taking any chances. It was a good thing, too, because once I heard a shell coming which sounded like it was going way over my head, but it landed about 25 feet from me. It just went "pop" and hit four fellows that were standing up. The Germans were throwing in all sizes of shells so it was hard to judge them all.

We finally made it to the town and wiped out what little resistance that was there. I was all out of breath and trembling like a leaf by that time. I found myself a nice comfortable spot to plunk down. I no sooner got situated when my squad leader called me and said we were going out on patrol. It seems as though we didn't meet too much resistance taking this town and the next one was only about half a mile away. So our commander wanted to send a patrol there to scout the place out. My squad was elected for the job. We were to move in and if there weren't any Germans there, we were to get back the best way we could.

We set out cautiously across another open field. There was a light hill that we had to go down. When we were on the forward slope, we found out that there were Germans in the next town and plenty of them. We all hit the ground as bullets started to crack over our heads. I thought this was the end. Here we were, on open ground on the forward slope of the hill with no cover at all. Our squad leader was an old hand at situations like this and immediately surveyed the land. He spotted a little cover about 50 yards from him.

He called the automatic rifleman to follow him. In the meantime, he told us to open up and shoot at anything that looked like anything. All the time the Germans were shooting all around us. As we opened up, the German shooting stopped. Red, the squad leader, ran over to the cover with the BAR (Browning automatic rifle). As soon as he got there he yelled back and told us to work our way back while he covered us with the BAR. Before we could move, one of the fellows was hit just as he started to move. I guess the Germans thought we were all hit when we hit the ground the first time, but when we started to move, they opened up on us again. Meantime, the fellow that got hit worked his way over to Red. They took care of his wound then tried to decide what to do next. The rest of us were still out in the open. Red told half of the squad to work its way back while the other half covered them with fire.

I was with the first half so I slowly turned around and started to move back. I had an awful time trying to crawl. The field was muddy and full of cornstalks. The cornstalks kept getting caught in my belt. It was a mess. I spotted a mound of earth about 100 yards back and started out for it. About half of the way there, someone must have spotted me because the bullets started to hit all around me. I didn't waste any more time then.

I got up and ran the rest of the way. Lord only knows why I wasn't hit. I yelled back that I made it. The other three made their spots, too.

So it was our turn to open up while the other three that covered us made their way back. Meanwhile, the two fellows that were with the wounded man devised a system whereby they held the BAR between them and the wounded man sat on it. They started out but a bullet knocked the BAR out from under him and he dropped it on the ground. Red and the other fellow dropped back to their own position. The wounded fellow started to take matters in his own hands. I guess he didn't want to us to endanger ourselves trying to get back to him, so he got up and, holding his stomach, started to run back to town. Bullets were kicking up all around him as he ran but he made it. By then, I had calmed down somewhat as I was now protected from the bullets. I was beginning to think that the Germans were pretty poor shots.

Red told us to stay in our positions and shoot it out. He knew that the company commander was mapping out some kind of move. Sure enough, here comes six of our tanks. The Germans saw them too and began to get out of their holes and run. I put my first notch in my rifle stock.

A half minute later after our tanks appeared, the Germans began to shell them. The tanks didn't stop, but kept going, firing into the town. As the tanks passed me in the field, eight Germans jumped out of their holes that weren't 50 yards away. Boy, if I'd known that they were that close to me, I would have fainted. Funny that they didn't fire at me. Maybe they were just as scared as I was.

The Germans must have started to move their artillery positions back because the shelling stopped and our company moved into town and cleared it out quickly.

Our squad took over a house that overlooked an important road crossing. A foxhole was about 25 yards up the same road that the Germans used for their retreat. Red decided that the foxhole was a good position to defend in the case of counterattack. It was known that the Germans had a couple of tanks and if they were going to use them, then they would have to come down the road. So after checking it out for booby traps, Red put two men in the hole with a bazooka.

There was a thick forest right next to the town we were in. The Germans had withdrawn into it. Our commander figured if there was going to be a counter-attack, it would come from the forest. He called up for artillery fire. While this was going on, it came my turn to move to the foxhole guard. When the artillery barrage came, it really came! The woods were only 50 yards from the hole and a lot of the shells came mighty close. As it was, the CO's suspicions were right because no sooner had the barrage lifted, out came quite a few Germans with white flags, hands up, and yelling "comrade" to the top of their voices. Another barrage brought more of them out.

The Germans must have figured we would occupy the house were in because of its strategic position. So they started to throw artillery at it. They threw in quite a lot of it too, but through some miracle not one of the shells hit the house.

I guess our artillery barrage into the nearby forest must have upset any plans that the Germans had for a counterattack, but we were all on the alert for one. We had a man at each window observing. Things quieted down later on. Then, real early in the morning, one of the fellows said he saw something moving in the field across the road. We all looked for a while and then decided he imagined it. Then about half an hour later, mortar shells started to fall all around the place. That fellow hadn't imagined anything after all and we let some Germans set up some mortars in the field. But it so happened that one of our tanks had pulled up for the night a few houses in the rear. The fellow they had on guard spotted the flash from the mortars. A few rounds from their 75mm gun made a mess out of them. For the rest of the night it was quiet. I managed to get one hour of sleep that night.

The next day, we got our new orders. Intelligence found out the Germans had built their final defense line in Alsace around Hagenau. It was the mission of our company to feel out these defenses and try to find a weak spot if we could.

We started out into the very woods that we had shelled the night before. We covered quite a bit of ground before we ran into a few snipers. They were quickly eliminated without stopping our advance at all. Then a little farther, we ran into more of them. We slowed down a little and moved more cautiously. At any movement, all hell was going to break loose. We knew it, but we had to keep moving. I could hear our tanks moving slowly behind us. Even as we advanced now and then, I heard someone yell "comrade" and some German would come out of his hole with his hands up, glad as all hell to give up rather than fight it out. Now and then one would choose to shoot it out, but they didn't last long afterwards.

Then it happened. We hit their first line of defense. It consisted mostly of riflemen, light machine guns and small mortars. Our causalities mounted rapidly until we were ordered to withdraw about 300 yards. We moved back and then to dig whatever protection we needed. Then it was the artillery's turn. They had been following our advance and know just where we were. It wasn't five minutes after we withdrew when the German positions were lambasted with shells and mortars.

About a half hour later, we started our advance again. We passed through the position easily. I saw then what artillery can do to a human body, but for some strange reason it didn't bother me one bit. I guess I had begun to get hardened to such things. This was only their first line of defense and we knew the next one would be tougher.

Later, I was told that I had become the ammunition bearer for the BAR. So in addition to my regular equipment, I had to carry a belt full of magazines for the BAR which weighed in the neighborhood of 24 pounds.

We came to a fire-lane in the forest and the first men to try to cross it were cut down by a machine gun the Germans had set up to the left of us. That held up our advance so a tank was called up to wipe out the nest if it could. We didn't have any "Commando Kellys" with us, so the tank was our choice. Up it came just as bold as anything, right across the fire-lane and let go with its cannon at the nest. Then all of a sudden, "Wham!" The tank was hit right smack in the center by an 88mm shell. After that, whatever the Germans had back there started to fire into our position, direct fire. Machine guns also opened up. Then almost as quick as it had started, it stopped. We heard equipment being moved, trucks moving and tanks roaring. "Here comes a counterattack," I thought. But instead of attacking, they were withdrawing. I guess they already had a taste of the artillery that was supporting us and didn't want any more of it. By that time our commander decided to stop our advance and hold our position that night. We dug in and rested. In the meantime, I was moved to assistant BAR man.

All through the night we could hear the Germans moving equipment around. I didn't know whether it was coming or going. Then once in a while they would try to send a patrol through our lines, but we drove them off each time.

It was foggy that morning and visibility was cut down to 75 yards. We sent out our patrols to scout out the front positions. We found them to be deserted. The Germans had withdrawn again. So we saddled up and moved forward. We moved quite a distance this time. Through thick forests, open clearings, and such, without meeting any resistance at all. Our company was well in advance of everything. Then while moving through a sort of finger of woods, our forward elements came upon some snipers, then later a machine gun. I was informed that I had become the BAR man and was issued the weapon. Before we could plan any movement to engage the machine gun, another one opened up on our left hand and then another one on our right flank. It became apparent that our company walked into a trap.

To top this all off, the Germans began to lay in artillery and mortars on us; first working on our rear to cut it off and then working on our forward positions. Let me tell you it was "hell first class!" I was behind a tree trying to make myself as inconspicuous as possible. It was here I got nicked on the hand. The fellow on my right was hit in the arm and leg, the fellow in back of me, "isn't here any more" and the one on my right is probably back in the States.

I couldn't reach back to get my shovel to dig in because I could see small twigs breaking off inches over my head and the bark on the tree I was behind was being chewed off from the bullets. So I started to dig with my hands. I dug a hole for my face and stuck it down into the hole. I put my hands in back of my helmet and held it down over my neck. It was then that a piece of shrapnel came along and nicked my hand and took half of my sleeve with it.

Our CO called for tanks once more to come up and at least stop the machine guns. Out of all the noise, I could hear the tanks coming. It's almost like the stories you read in books where in comes the hero to the rescue. Slowly, they came firing their machine guns and blasting away with their cannons at the German machine guns. They must have scored some hits because the Germans stopped firing shortly after. The artillery was still coming in but at least we could get up and dig some sort of shelter for ourselves. I knew darn well we weren't going to advance any farther, so I just dug and dug.

Later on their artillery let up a little and we eased up a bit, too. Another night passed without much sleep because we were busy guarding against any counterattacks and chasing off German patrols.

About 8 A.M. the next morning, they started to shell our position again. It lasted for over six hours without let up. When it finally let up, we were ordered to move back the best we could and fast (that is, what was left of us).

We started to move back between barrages. We moved back 800 yards and dug in but good, two men to a hole. We dug the holes deep and covered them with thick logs and at least 18 inches of dirt. It was protection from everything but a direct hit. About 400 yards farther back was a mansion of a farmhouse where we got extra blankets to line our foxholes.

We had hit the main line of defense and found out its strength and position and now it was up to our artillery to soften it up a bit before we could advance any farther.

They told us that we may have to stay in this position for a little while so we started to make things more comfortable. My buddy and I went to work enlarging our hole a bit and touching things up. I managed to get a couple of sofa pillows to put on the bottom of the hole and also a kerosene lamp. I took a one gallon can that I found and made a cover out of it after I dug out a place in the side of the foxhole. The kerosene lamp furnished the heat. I baked mostly the cheese and crackers out of my K Dinner Unit in the oven. But once I managed to bake a small chicken in it which didn't turn out too bad.

The farmhouse had a very large stock of canned goods: string beans, lima beans, spinach, carrots, cherries, pears, peaches, and strawberries, not to mention many varieties of jams and jellies. I forgot to mention the grape wine they had, but every farmhouse had wine in their cellars, so it wasn't unusual. All in all, we were very fortunate to have stopped by such a place.

We stayed there about six days while our artillery worked on the German positions. During this time, we sent our numerous patrols to spot out different positions the Germans might have established. Then, once in a while, we would organize a combat patrol to go out and try to get prisoners for questioning. This was a very ticklish job. The combat patrol that I went on, went out early in the morning before sunrise. We walked up to a certain point where we thought the German outposts might be and then split up in three groups of four men each. Then we would slowly advance until we spotted one of them. Usually around this time of the morning, nine chances out of ten, everyone is dozing off to sleep, even the guards that are supposed to be awake. I was actually amused to witness such a thing.

Another fellow and I approached the hole that was "V" shaped with two Germans in it. Both were sound asleep. We put our bayonets on and then placed them right on the throats of each German. One of them raised his hand and pushed my bayonet away in his sleep like a person would brush away a fly. I placed it back on his throat again and pressed down a little. He opened his eyes and just stared at me.

Suddenly, he realized what was going on and turned white as a sheet. The fellow that was with me woke up his man in the same manner. Both Germans just laid there not moving a muscle. My buddy put a finger to his lips and motioned them to get up out of their hole quietly. They were more than willing to go. Our patrol managed to get four prisoners that way, without firing a shot. It just goes to show how dangerous it is to fall asleep at your post.

The very same thing has happened to men on our outposts. Sometimes you will be just standing there and doze off without even knowing it. One night one of our officers came up and took a fellow's rifle away right out from his hands. He called a couple of times before the soldier answered. The officer asked him if he was asleep and the fellow seemed very disturbed at being accused of being asleep. He denied it bitterly. Then the officer asked him where his rifle was. You can figure out the rest. I hate to go into it any further.

Well, getting back to the story again. We were in this position for six days. On the sixth day, another company tried to get through the German defenses but was beaten back. There happened to be a long zigzag trench the Germans had dug and protected it stubbornly. Our artillery worked on the position and the company made another attempt which failed. On the seventh day, our company was then given the job of taking this position. We were to push off at seven in the morning under an artillery barrage and follow the barrage right up to the trench and then jump in with bayonets fixed and dig them out.

At seven that morning, the artillery opened up and we followed up behind the barrage as planned. I was sacred as hell! This was going to be my first hand-to-hand combat, maybe, and I didn't like it one bit. We advanced to within 50 yards of the trench and waited till the barrage let up. Then we charged the position yelling like mad and jumped in. To our great joy, we found the trench to be deserted. Not a German was there. Some of the fellows were so relieved they just bawled like babies. But the joy was short-lived, as the Germans knew we were there and started to pound the place with their own artillery.

Here's where another miracle happened. They probably threw in from 300 to 400 shells and not one of them landed in the trench. Some of them landed close enough to cave in the sides here and there, but not one man was hit.

We stayed there in the trench the rest of the day waiting for further orders but we didn't get any. I guess the big shots were gathering all the information on the day's fighting as we weren't the only ones participating. About 10 that evening, we were to withdraw from our position for some reason. We went all the way back to our former positions where we pushed off that morning. Most of the fellows were sort of mad to give up this land. I was one of them. Here one company loses a lot of men trying to take it, and then our company manages to get there, only to withdraw. It didn't make any sense. But that night we found out but quick. The Germans plastered the spot with artillery for about three straight hours without letup.

Early the next morning, we cautiously went back and occupied the place again. It didn't look the same at all. That trench was really blasted out. I didn't know how the big shots figured that move out, but from then on, we didn't question any of their moves.

While this was going on, another part of our regiment moved around to another section and managed to get Hagenau, France, from the flanks. When the Germans moved to stop them, we pushed into town from our sector. I might add that Harry, who was in the other attacking unit, was one of the first to get into the city. As a matter of fact, his machine gun squad was in one of the houses a whole day before the rest of his company got in. He was even caught under his own artillery barrage while he was there. They didn't know anyone had made it. It was pretty rough going for him that first day.

I guess by then the Germans figured it was useless to defend the place any more and made a quick retreat. We spent the night in Hagenau drinking up the good beer and wine and celebrating with the newly liberated people. They were really happy to see us. You should have seen them. As we marched through the streets (not a parade but in tactical formation, ten yards between each man just in case of snipers), the people gave us the good old Army solute and waved French flags for the first time in several years. What was amusing was to watch the little tots. They didn't know any other army but the German. So, as we passed by they snapped to attention and gave out with the Heil Hitler salute. Their parents quickly slapped their hands and from the tone of their voices, I could just imagine what they were saying. The poor kids didn't know what it was all about but they were quick to find out that we had chocolate on us and soon were pestering the life out of us. Of course we were used to this by now and took it in stride.

We spent two days in Hagenau, a good time but most of us caught up on our sleep. The beds we had were a far cry from the foxholes we had spent a week in.

The third day we pulled out again to catch up with the Germans. We hiked 10 miles without anything happening. That night we slept in a small village in beds again.

The next day we boarded tanks and rode for about another 20 miles. This brought us right up to the German border.

We stayed in a small town for two days while patrols were sent out across the border to scout around. There were thick forests and the scenery was really beautiful. The patrols spotted a couple of pill-boxes and reported them. The next day, we loaded up with pole and satchel charges (used to knock out pill-boxes), and pushed off into Germany. The pill-boxes which were spotted turned out to be empty, much to our relief, so we kept going. Shortly after, we ran into some resistance again. It was pretty rough, but I'm not going into detail about it. We hit the dragon's teeth of the Siegfried Line and were stopped cold. After withdrawing slightly, we dug in and remained in the woods for two days. This is when we got the news of the German breakdown in Belgium. Our commander decided to withdraw and wait for further developments. So we moved down to Lauterbourg where we built up a defense line with outposts along the Rhine River. We spent about 10 days there.

Christmas and New Year passed. Things were relatively quiet. The Germans only sent in shells between 7:30 to 8:00 A.M. and 6:00 to 6:30 every day. We could almost set our watches by it.

I had dozed off in a foxhole dug there. It was located in an old cemetery. My buddy and I dug it deep and wide. We had a one-sixteenth-inch steel plate for a roof that was supported by steel beams and had about 20 inches of dirt piled on top of that that froze solid from the cold. We lined the interior with pressed cork slabs that we found in a nearby building. On the bottom, we laid the cushion from the studio couch.

We dug out one corner and lined it with bricks and placed a small stove there. A smoke pipe was run underground for about 20 yards away from our hole and then coming up through the bush. And that's the way things were for 10 days. We spent 18 hours a day just watching across the Rhine. We went into the town for each meal but we spend each night guarding.

During this time, quite a few German patrols came over to scout out our positions. On some of these patrols, a few of them would break away and desert, giving themselves up to us. We found out from them that something was in the wind and was due any day now. Here's where the big shots pulled another smart move.

They figured that because the Germans were doing well up north, they might try the same thing here. We withdrew our forces and built up a very strong line from Hatendown to

Strasbourg passing by Haguenau. Then the Germans came. They formed a huge pincer move from the north around Hatten and south just above Strasbourg.

I can imagine their big surprise when they found we weren't caught in the move. They hit our line hard. They managed to make some progress, but it was costly. Then it was our turn to move. We were in Bischwiller at the time and the Germans had just taken the town only 1.5 miles away. We planned to counter-attack the next day. It was the 7th of January, 1945. But this is where I'll have to close for now, because the story goes into another phase. And besides, this letter is getting pretty big. I'll continue at a later date. So long for now, dear. I love you.

Hubby

Part 2

We were to launch an attack against a town called Rohrwiller. There was a large field we had to cross and we had planned to use smoke to cover our attack. The morning turned out to be foggy, which was a break for us. We had 18 tanks, so part of the attacking force rode on top of them until resistance was met. I was one in a group that rode on a tank. I sat just behind the turret with my BAR.

The time for the attack approached rapidly. It looked like the start of a big race.

The tanks were lined up 75 yards apart. The command tank was in the middle. Behind the line of tanks were the foot troops. Then the commanding officer gave the signal to start. The air was filled with the roar of the motors as the tanks slowly started to move.

My heart was racing like the devil as I looked straight ahead, trying to see through the thick fog. You'd be surprised to know some of the thoughts that go through a man's head at a time like this, not knowing what that fog might be concealing ahead of us.

We went slowly, not more that 3-5 miles-per-hour. We expected an artillery barrage to come in on us as was so common in almost all our previous attacks.

We rode and rode. Then the commander ordered a halt. I guess he was going to use a different plan of attack as we had met no resistance so far. Then he ordered us on again, but this time we went full speed ahead. I had all I could do to hang on. The tank in which I was riding went down a small depression in the ground and came up with a bound. When it came down, I went down with it, but my helmet was riding a straight line and as a result, I lost it. I really felt naked, but then one of the tankers gave me his to wear so I felt better again.

One of the fellows poked me and hollered, "There they are!" I strained my eyes through the fog and sure enough there they were. But luckily someone had better eyes than us and discovered they were civilian, so we held our fire. They were all out in the open yelling and waving their arms trying to stop us so they could tell us something. We stopped and they told us there were about 40 Germans in town that might put up a fight. The civilians went on to tell us where they were.

Everyone got off the tanks and cautiously approached the houses that were pointed out to them. Three other fellows and I were going through a yard and between two houses, when a man came up and told us there were two Germans guarding a small bridge. We went over to get them. Cautiously, we sneaked up behind the last house facing the bridge. Sure enough, there they were, standing up in their holes on the other side of the stream without their helmets. We thought they wanted to give up being they had their helmets off. We slowly approached them. Pete, one of the fellows, walked right up the middle of the road approaching the bridge. He got to within 25 feet of the bridge and hesitated for a moment. Just then the bridge blew up. Pete reeled back from the explosion and immediately dropped to one knee and started to fire at the two Germans. By this time, they had ducked down into their holes. Then up popped one of them and fired a rifle grenade right at Pete. I looked up and found Pete still on one knee. He looked over to me and pointed to the hole in front of him and yelled, "Kellman, did you see that!? Those bastards want to kill me!" He then ran back and got behind a cement wall and started firing again.

All four of us had dropped back to some sort of cover and started firing. By this time, the tanks that were with us heard all the noise and three of them came up to help the situation out. Pete seemed to be the one the Germans had picked out because every time he fired a shot, they wouldn't fire just a bullet at him, but a rifle grenade. Shortly, there wasn't much left of the wall he was behind, so he had to find another. Each time a grenade would explode against the wall, he let out with a loud "Yowey!"

The tanks came up and we showed them where the Germans were holed up. One of the tanks stayed behind while the other two drove right up to the bank of the stream and let go with a round of H.E. from their 76mm cannons. We thought that finished them off but a few seconds later, one popped up with a bazooka and fired it at one of the tanks. The rocket missed and hit a house nearly blowing the whole side in. The German bazookas are really wicked. After that, the tanks fired two rounds at them. Up one popped again and fired a rifle grenade this time. It hit one of the tanks but didn't do any serious damage. This time the tanks pumped about five or six rounds apiece at the hole. By then, the rest of the German outfit started to lay in mortars around our position. They were behind a factory across the stream about 100 yards away. We all ran for cover but the tanks held their positions. I guess the two Germans in the hole decided to make a run for it but when they jumped out of their hole, our tanks cut them down with their machine guns. I sort of admired their courage—standing their ground against two tanks.

That was the only fight that had gone on in the whole town as the rest of the Germans gave up willingly. Shortly after our outfit moved into town, the Germans started to shell it heavily, but soon quieted down.

Taking this town was the objective of our company and we made it without much trouble. Two other companies in our battalion were to take the next town. They met up with a little more resistance so we helped up for a while till we heard that they had gotten into town finally. We then followed up and were to clean out a patch of woods before going into town. We were told that there probably wasn't anything in there and it would be just a routine mop up. In we went, cautiously but not too worried. Sure enough nothing was happening. We went through rather quickly and crossed over a railroad track—that is, part of us did. As we were crossing, a machine gun opened up on our right, firing down the tracks.

I don't know how many got hit because I was one of the few that made it across the tracks. The firing came from a house about 100 yards down the tracks. Some of the fellows stayed behind on the other side of the tracks and moved up on the house while those of us that got across engaged the nest in a fire fight. The Germans didn't want to fight very hard for one of them gave up while the other ran away. Then another machine gun opened up on us from further down the tracks, so we brought up our 60mm mortars and plastered the position good. That was the finish for that machine gun.

Then all hell broke loose on us again. I guess we had stumbled on the Germans that had planned to counterattack our other two companies. So instead, they launched their attack on us.

They had a couple of S.P. (self propelled) guns with them and opened them up on us. They fired at the trees about 6 to 10 feet off the ground and were very accurate. Men all over were getting hit! I lost my assistant gunner and ammunition bearer from the first burst which was directly over their heads. After the S.P. barrage, they laid in artillery and heavy mortars on us. Then came their infantry, yelling like mad and firing wildly in every direction. Our mortars saved the day for us because they started to lay them in the German positions as soon as they had opened up. I guess the rounds were accurate for as soon as they started to land, everything quieted down with only a shot now and then. We could hear the wounded Germans moaning and screaming like the devil. I have yet to hear a GI carry on as much as a German when he is wounded.

We withdrew back across the tracks, taking our wounded with us, and started to dig in for the night. We could hear all kinds of machines moving around in front of us. The Germans were up to something and we had to find out what. We sent out a patrol to do a little spying. The patrol came back and said they saw the Germans pulling out. We rested a little easier after that.

We got word that the other two companies had taken the whole town and were holding against only slight resistance. Our C.O. decided to have us move in and rest there for the night.

The other two companies were in one part of the town while we were in the lower part. There was a small stream running through the place dividing it evenly. It was planned that tomorrow the other companies were to push off at 7 A.M. and take the next one. We didn't have any mission, so we were going to "sleep in."

January 8, 1945

The morning came and there was a lot of noise. Naturally, we thought this was the other companies going into the attack but looking at our watches, we saw that it was only 5 a.m. Something went wrong. Sure enough, in came a runner and told us that the Germans were counterattacking with several tanks (Tigers), armored infantry, S.S., and paratroopers. The other companies weren't capable of holding so they were waiting for support so they could withdraw. We were immediately rushed to their part of town and held up by the river to cover their withdrawal. There was a lot of confusion in the moments that followed. The main street made a 30 degree bend before it crossed the stream so we were able to move up pretty close without being spotted. The tanks that were supporting were withdrawing fast, driving backward with their guns blazing away at the Germans coming up the street from the far side of town. The German tanks hadn't shown up yet, but they were doing plenty of shooting. The men from the other companies started to withdraw to a position behind our lines to blast the small bridge that crossed the stream. They didn't destroy it, but weakened it so none of the German tanks could get across.

The Germans moved to the edge of the stream and put up positions in the houses along the way. That's the way the situation was for a few hours. Our platoon leader picked two men from our squad to take up positions in the house that looked down the street into the German positions. They did and were having a pretty good time picking off Germans that moved carelessly out in the open. They sniped away for several hours before the Germans finally located their spot. Then came a Tiger tank right up to the bridge and blasted away at the house. The first round must have been a dud because it went right through the place; one thick outer wall, two inner walls and through the other outer wall. That first round was enough to convince the fellows that the house wasn't a very healthy place any more. They vacated, but quick. After that, the tank pumped 10 or 15 rounds into the house, nearly leveling it. In the mean. The crew jumped out and managed to get away. The others were cut down by our machine guns.

Night came in on us with the situation as described. Things quieted down a bit. We were able to get our rations and load up with ammo. We mapped out a plan in which we were to draw up some artillery and blast the part of the town the Germans occupied. After that, we would cross the bridge and take a couple of houses on the other side of the stream. We all tried to get some sleep that night.

The next morning, we were all set to go when we discovered that the Germans got through our lines and were in amongst us. That was the payoff. From that moment on, it was every man for himself. There was plenty of confusion, just like one of those gang fights you see in the western movies. In a short time, I became separated from my unit and was on my own. I had only 12 magazines for my BAR, which totaled 240 rounds. That wasn't very much for a fight of that sort.

As I said before, I lost my assistant and ammo bearer, so I was short. I took up a position in a yard that overlooked a small field. I spotted some Germans that were trying to get across this field from behind a house. Every time they started out, I fired a burst at them. I don't think I got any of them but I kept them back. They tried to go around the other side of the house, but I spotted them again and this time, I winged a couple. I fired again but my BAR jammed. I decided to get out of this place in a hurry. I turned and started up the rear stairs of a house that I was behind. Just then a mortar hit the roof of the house and as I closed the door, another mortar hit the steps that I had just used. The blast blew the glass in the door in my face and blew me across the room against the opposite wall.

As I sat against the wall, a civilian came up from the basement to see what the noise was all about. He spotted me across the room and then helped me to the basement. There were 16 people down there and a Catholic priest. The priest came over to me and gave me last rites . . . ha! I stayed down in that basement for about four hours while all the shooting was going on outside. Then when things quieted down, I decided to go outside and find my outfit. If the Germans had control of the town, I would surrender. I became more alarmed because I didn't remember the password for that night. I could be shot by my own men! I started calling, "Any GIs around here?" (I later found out that this was an old German trick.) Luckily, nobody shot at me. Finally, I spotted a pin-point of light coming from a hole in the basement. I pushed the door open only to find the muzzle of two MI's stuck in my face. Then I heard someone say, "Hey! It's a GI!"

They took me down to the basement where there was nearly a whole platoon from the 42nd. Division. A lieutenant came up to me and ask me how it was going up there. I said, "Don't you know!"

He said, "Hell no! We've been down here for two days."

He told me that he would try to contact my unit by radio. He was successful and my outfit sent a jeep over to pick me up. The medic took a look at my condition. The eyelid to my left eye were peeled back behind the eyeball. It made my eye appear as though it was out of its socket. The medic dabbed the eye with some pain-deadening solution. I was then put in an ambulance and sent to the rear. I later learned that it was the last ambulance that had gotten out of that town.

After getting out of the hospital, I went through the replacement system again. The place I finally ended up at was in the Vosges Mountains. The name of the place was Wagonberg. That's the place where I told you I had such a nice time. While I was there, I got news that our battalion no longer existed. The Germans were too strong for them. They cut them off and had them surrounded for 6 or 7 days. What was finally left of the outfit surrendered. Yep, that's what happened, wiped out. All of my buddies, gone. I was stunned at the news. Those things happen in wartime.

In the days that followed, one by one various fellows made their way back to our lines after the surrender. They had all sorts of stories to tell. Some good, some not so good. A total of 90 men had gotten away from the Germans and made their way back. It was around these men that the new battalion was formed. That's how I got my Staff Sergeants rating. I was one of the "old" fellows. In the next couple of weeks, the replacements started to come in. Soon we were up to full strength again with new equipment, etc. We trained together for a short period and had numerous orientations in which some of the "older fellows" gave some pointers on combat.

Finally, we were all ready and pulled out to the front lines again. By this time, the Germans had made some progress and had Haguenau all but surrounded. As a matter of fact, they were in half of Haguenau with the Moder River separating us. We moved into Haguenau but stayed in the rear area, about 1,000 yards behind the lines. We stayed there for several days not doing a thing but sitting around listening to the noise of battle. Once in a while, we would form a patrol and go through some patches of woods that the Germans might have dropped para-troopers in for some surprise raid or something.

Then after a time, we were ordered to pack all our equip-ment to move. Instead of going to the front lines, we moved away from it. We walked back about 5 miles to another town and settled down for the rest. It was then that we found out that our whole division was being pulled out of the line for a break. Everybody was sure glad to hear that news.

That next day, we all piled on trucks ready to move out. While we were waiting to pull out, some Germans flew over in 4 of our own P-47 planes and started to strafe some artillery posi-tions. We were only 1,000 yards from this and it sure gave us all a scare! But they only shot at artillery positions and didn't even bother us. We would have been dead ducks if they had.

We moved out and drove way back to a little town called Belleville, which is just a short distance from Nancy. It was there that I got my pass to Nancy. While on pass, I enjoyed things so much. It was nice to be away from all the noise of battle. About two three hours later, 3 buzz-bombs fell on the city—yowey! At first, I thought it might be some engineers blowing us some wreckage. Then the second one came in. I noticed the people running for the air-raid shelters. Before I woke up to the fact, the third one came in and landed only 2 blocks away. I was al-most knocked off my feet by the jar. Wham!

From Belleville, we moved up to Diepenbeek, Belgium, after nine days. We stayed there for six days. On the 5th day, we were informed that we were now in the 9th Army and were elected to be one of the landing units on the Roer River assault (nice honor). Our regiment was the only one in the division to be committed at this time. Our plans were to attack a place that was over 80 miles from where we were. We pulled out by truck and approached our place of assembly. We arrived at the point of departure, just before the time of attack. Everything went okay. We got there about 1 A.M., two and a half hours before the attack. We waited around nervously, getting our final instructions and checking our equipment. The town we were to attack was only 800 yards away and we could just see it in the moonlight.

At 3 a.m., the artillery was supposed to open up and last for 45 minutes. On February 23, 1945, at three on the button, the artillery opened up. I had never heard such a barrage in my life. They really had the guns up here; a lot more than what the 7th Army had. You know how applause sounds? Well, just imagine

Norman Kellman(left) and his captain, Paul Hurst

cannons being fired that rapidly and you'll have some idea how it sounded.

The minutes ticked away quickly. The artillery increased in intensity. After 45 minutes was up, the artillery ceased. We pushed off. Zip! That's how fast we went into town. Nobody there, except what was left of some animals. The German soldiers weren't there. But in the next town, a short distance away, another company met some machine gun fire that chased them across a mine field. They had quite a few casualties. We hastily set up defense positions making ready for any counterattack. None came, so we relaxed. We found out later that we were in on the big push to the Rhine. But we only had to clean out a few towns west of the Roer and our job was finished. The big-shots had something big for us in the future. The other divisions had the job of cleaning up the territory west of the Rhine, while we stayed in Berg, near the Roer. Berg is near Kerchhoven, which is in turn near Heinsberg. Heinsberg is the largest place, so I think it will be easier to find on a map. Look for Roermond, Holland, and you'll get the general location if you move east from there.

We stayed there for about a week and then pulled out and moved to a town by the name of Beeck, Germany. We stayed there about 5 days and had the job of cleaning out bypassed areas and searching out mine fields. Nothing much happened during this operation.

We then packed up again and pulled back to Holland. This is where I had such a pleasant stay. The name of the place was Orsbeek, which is near Herleen.

Our main reason for moving back there was to take amphibious training for the big push across the Rhine. We stayed there for two weeks, to train.

Then came the time for us to pull out. We moved by trucks into Germany once more to a small town. I don't remember the place now, but it wasn't very far from Rhineburg. We stayed there two days while we watched thousands of bombers going and coming across the river, dropping their bombs about 10 miles from where we were.

On the third day, we were given final instructions on the Rhine crossing, that was about to take place. We pulled out that evening and moved to the point of departure under cover of darkness and dug in for the night. We were about 2 miles from the river, in front of our artillery positions.

Everything was peaceful at first. Nothing but the continuous drone of airplane motors as they kept up their bombing attacks. Then at midnight, our artillery opened up. It was a terrific barrage. More terrible than the Toer push-off. The sky was lit up in an almost continuous flash. I read later that this was the most terrific artillery barrage in history. This barrage kept up for 4 hours. At 6 A.M., we pushed off. I was in charge of eight men, Our number was gray seven, and we were to get into boat 13 for the crossing. When we got to the river, there was a large dike which our engineers dug a passage through and instead of the regular assault boats which we had trained in, they had large amphibious trucks, called "alligators." The actual crossing was a picnic.

We moved in for almost a mile, then dug in, in a large field. We stayed there waiting for our armored support to come across.

The Germans were waiting for it and shot an 88 at the tanks. The shot missed, came across the field and hit a tree near my foxhole. A piece of the shell hit me in the face.

Our division, the 79th, suffered only 30 causalities. I was one of the 30.

Carl G. Campbell

79th Infantry Division, 314th Regiment, 2nd Battalion
Prisoner of War

I was born in Luverene, Alabama, the oldest of three children. I graduated from high school in the spring of 1942, and on November 1, 1943, entered the Army at Fort Bragg, North Carolina. After having completed basic training at Camp Wheeler, Georgia, I was given a few days before reporting to Fort Meade, Maryland. After spending three or four days there, I was sent on to Camp Myles Standish, Massachusetts, where the entire 79th was ready for a move to Europe.

The voyage across the Atlantic was via the SS *Strathmoore*, a British ship. It was filthy and we were only served two meals a day. After docking, we spent an extra day on the ship, then were moved by train to a tent city located on a golf course, some forty miles east of Liverpool, England. A few days before the invasion, we made our trip south to another tent city to await the big day.

My training had included the M-I converter, a decoding device for messages, and I was introduced to the technique of laying telephone wire and other activities of the wire section. When we received word of D-Day, we had already begun waterproofing all our gear and only two or three days later we were on our way to Plymouth and ready for the overnight trip to France.

After landing in France, we immediately cleared the beach and stopped to take all the waterproofing of of the vehicles and

Carl G. Campbell, 1940s.

personnel equipment. This was D-Day plus eight days. Two days later, we had moved through some uncharted areas and put on line between the 90th and the 4th divisions. The next few days and nights we spent getting used to all types of live fire, and moving toward Cherbourg, clearing the peninsula.

One day after the fall of Cherbourg, France, it was off to the east, and preparations were made for the outbreak. Thick hedgerows were everywhere. On the 7th of July, we moved into a hedgerow located on the forward slope of a hill with the line company about 200 yards and facing the road. A deep gully lined with small trees and brush led downhill to this road. The strong odor of powder was in the air, and I realized that our artillery had caught up with them. There were body parts everywhere. I don't know how many Germans there were because I don't recall ever seeing a whole body. This sight made me physically sick even though they were the enemy. When you see humans blown apart, regardless of nationality, empty feelings take root and last a long time. Most units recover their dead as soon as possible and never leave them for graves registration. However, during this period, one dead GI was sitting upright, leaning on a bank, his rifle across his lap. A sad sight. Across the road, the terrain began to rise for a couple of miles. La Haye du Puits was just east of our position. Our line company had attacked the Jerries across the road in front of us. We were not successful and returned to our former positions.

About noon the next day, July 8, we began receiving direct fire from 88s on the high ground in front of us. The fire was accurate and fierce. About 6:00 P.M., Captain Pasternak, the BN S-I emerged from the CP and ordered us to move back up the gully to positions held by the other GIs, three days before the 88s shelled us. We began receiving small arms fire before we could take up our positions. This was grazing fire coming from our left flank.

As we retreated to an area where the land was not sloping forward, we took foxhole positions our troops had held two days before. I was in a two-man foxhole when I felt a sudden urge to have a bowel movement. I don't know if my nervous state caused this, but I was behind a hedgerow and anxious to return to my foxhole. I was standing near my foxhole, my rifle between my knees, tightening my belt, when I felt a blow to my right leg. I glanced at my pants leg and found what appeared to be a knife slit. My foxhole buddy urged me into the foxhole. I pulled all three pairs of pants down past my knees and found a wound about the size of a pencil. We called the medics and were told to get to a safer place to be treated, about fifty yards away.

Here the medics cut all my clothes from my leg, covered the wound with sulfur powder, bandaged the wound, and filled out a causality slip. During the day, HQ-2-314 received 28 casualties, and I had been the last one, when I was hit in the right knee. The bullet was still in my leg, but I wasn't losing any blood. I was transferred through about four hospitals during the night and arrived at an evacuation hospital in the beach area very early on the morning of July 9. My leg became very painful, even from the movement of my stretcher. About 8:00 A.M., preparations were made to start moving the wounded out. I was placed on a C-47, filled with stretchers for the flight to Birmingham, England.

We arrived there about noon and were placed in wards where we got baths and clean pajamas. Later in the day, we were put in a stretcher line (one long line), which ran through x-ray, and then we had to wait for the operating rooms.

The operating room was vast and there must have been at least thirty teams working there. When I was wheeled to my place, the doctor already had the x-rays and was ready to remove the bullet from underneath my kneecap. The wound was not closed but was allowed to heal from the inside and later would be cleaned out and allowed to heal at the surface. The doctor gave me the bullet, which I have to this day.

Returning to the hospital after surgery, we were given a hot meal as soon as we were able to eat. The next day, July 10, we were loaded onto a hospital train and transported to a station hospital in South Wales to recover. I was not able to leave the hospital until about the first of October, over three months after being wounded. I was moved from several replacement depots, finally to arrive at HQ-2-314, around Thanksgiving Day 1944. It seems that they had just cleared Sarrebourg and the Saverne Pass.

It was certainly nice to see that most of the men in the unit were still safe. The action was fast and furious. We captured one company of Germans. We moved north through Bishwiller, Hagenau, and Ritershoffen, France. We crossed into Germany and spent Christmas 1944 in a small village. A day or two after Christmas, it became evident that a considerable amount of troop movement was going on with the Germans.

HQ-2-314 had an outpost about ten miles from the BNCP (battalion command post), which had the TD (tank destroyer), and a platoon of infantry controlling a bridge over a stream. As it became evident that we faced a defensive situation, this outpost requested pole charges of TNT, to blow the bridge upon withdrawal. It became my duty and another GI's to make the night trip to this outpost to carry the pole charges and bring back a dead GI.

It was only two days later that trucks arrived and all units moved south all night, taking up positions to defend a German bridgehead, held across the Rhine north of Strasbourg. HQ-2-314 spent the next several days in Drusenheim. Increased German activity was observed every day.

Finally, on the night of January 19, 1945, the Jerries attacked from the northeast, south, and southwest, surrounding three companies of the BN. The encircled troops were taken POW during the morning hours. It was about 1,000 yards from Drusenheim to the Rhine, and en route, all POWs were put upstairs in a large barn. It seems we were there two days with little or nothing to eat. We were then marched to the Rhine River, where we were put on a hand-operated ferry, the likes of which I have never seen, to cross the river, and then came the twenty-mile march in twelve inches of snow to our first POW camp.

The rail systems in Germany were a wreck. Bombing, American by day and British by night, left the system in such terrible conditions. Our move from Offenburg, France, to Ludwigsburg should have taken a few hours. Instead, it took twenty-four hours. The small openings on each end and on opposite sides of the boxcars were our only way of knowing what was going on outside. On each end and the top of the boxcar were two perches. This was where the guards rode.

As we got on the train, I noticed that the cars were not marked, and as the trains carried other boxcars, it would appear as a freight train. We were loaded and got away late in the afternoon. The train jerked and stopped all night. I can assure you that the trip was under conditions which allowed no sleep, and to add to this, there was no heat except that provided by our bodies.

Just past daybreak the next morning, the slow train came to a screeching halt. Our observers to the outside let us know that the entire train crew, including our quarts, could be seen running to the patch of woods about 200 yards away. "Our eyes" on the other end of the boxcar reported P-47s dive-bombing the village that we had just passed through! Being that the train was stopped, we could hear the planes coming close and we were doing some fast praying that they didn't attack our train.

It was with great joy that the train crew got back. The guards returned to their perches and we were on our way again. The train arrived at Stuttgart, Germany, in the afternoon. The door was unlocked and opened by the guards for some reason that I do not remember. I do remember that a German soldier gave us the word that FDR (Franklin D. Roosevelt) had died the day before. We had only a few miles to go and arrived in Ludwigsburg, Germany, our living quarters, which were very crude but a bit better than our first trip in Offenburg. Personally, I would not recommend a trip like this for a person with a weak heart.

It is difficult to remember dates and to determine just how long we stayed in any one of these camps. It seems to me that we had been in Ludwigburg for two or three weeks before I found myself ill with a very high fever. My friends urged me to go to the medics in the afternoon, even though the sick call was every morning. Well, I went and of course was advised that sick call was in the A.M. After some urging, he took my temperature, which was 103 degrees plus. He told me to get ready to go to the hospital. Awhile later, I was escorted to the hospital. After passing through the admitting office, I was directed to the fourth (top) floor and told to take a bunk. This I did and have never felt so sick in my life!

About an hour later, an air raid siren went off. At this point, I was so sick that I felt like I would be better off if the place was bombed. Just about that time, an armed German soldier came running through the ward and gave me a "special invitation" to go to the basement. Of course, there was only one stairway. Reaching the basement, there was no place to sit except on the floor. I also learned quickly the Frenchmen lived on floors one, two, and three. During any air raids, they carried all belongings, usually two suitcases or a small trunk. I soon figured out that these people in civilian clothes had surrendered with all their belongings.

I found a small place on the floor where I could sit and work my way into leaning against the wall. I guess the air raid lasted about one and a half hours. When the all-clear sounded, there was a rush for the stairs. As for myself, my fever turned into a chill and I did not feel like getting into a crowd. Previously, I had not had any symptoms of dysentery. It did, however, make me aware of my problem as soon as I started up stairs. I found a bathroom equipped with cold water, hand soap, and a place to wash clothes. The clothing I was wearing consisted of long underwear, OD woolens (dress uniform), and chemically treated fatigues. To make the story shorter, I proceeded to wash my clothes. Since I had no pajamas or other hospital clothing, I put my unsoiled clothing back on and put the other out to dry.

Finally, when a medic did come to check on me, I was given about three ounces of castor oil. He explained that this was crude, but the only medication he had. He said that it should eliminate the cause. Two nights later, he came by and gave me a handful of powdered charcoal, explaining that this would put the lining back in my stomach and intestines. During this time, he said I could have no food, but I couldn't have eaten anything anyway. Of all my experiences, including being wounded and captured, this was the most devastating. I felt helpless, useless—death almost a wel-

MSG Campbell, 1976

come end. After eight days, I was able to return and most happy to be with my friends. It was only two days later that we were moved to Moosburg, Germany, forty miles northeast of Munich.

All of these POW camps were very crude. Most had no place to sleep except on the floor. If you had a bunk, it was always a double and consisted of wood shavings stuffed into a burlap sack. In these conditions, body lice had their heyday. This condition was horrible at Moosburg, especially when we had to make three or four trips a night to the latrine (outdoors). At night we only took off our boots, because just about the time we would get to sleep, those bugs would start to work on us. Around the belt area or anyplace where the blood was near the surface of the skin was the favorite spot for them to dig in. Sometimes I could scratch and feel the blood splatter. "That's one gone but no way to get them all." It's a wonder I didn't die.

James R. Young (right).

James R. Young

United States Navy
USS *Heywood*

The Bronze Citation

In the name of the President of the United States, the
Commander in Chief, the Commander in Chief of the United
States Pacific Fleet, presents the Bronze Star Medal to Ensign
James R. Young, United States Navy Reserve for service as set
forth in the following citation:

Citation

For meritorious achievement as boat officer in the first assault
wave of LVT's from an attack transport in the assault on Tarawa.
He performed his duties with outstanding courage in the face of
enemy gunfire which hit the LVT in which he was embarked. His
conduct throughout was in keeping with the highest traditions of
the Naval service.

The LVT (landing vehicle tank) was destroyed. Of the 33
onboard, only three of us survived. Our ship's captain wrote in
for a Silver Star award but in the mass confusion of the time, it
was awarded to a fellow boat officer who was on LCVP, which was
hit but had no casualties. LCVP stood for "landing craft vehicle
and personnel," and it was an American-designed amphibious

tractor also known as "amphibious assault vehicle seven" (AAV-7A1). Both my knees were permanently damaged. I received 40 percent service-connected disability in the Tarawa landing.

• • •

James Young, a boat wave officer, was onboard the USS *Heywood,* an attack transport, on June 5, 1944. His ship spent World War II landing U.S. troops on enemy shores during the heat of battle in assault of enemy-held beaches. His crew of over 500 shipmates and a battalion of over 1,500 assault troops landed in Iceland in March 1942. The ship was later transferred to the Pacific. On June 5, 1944, the *Heywood,* headed westward in the mid-Pacific, was approaching the International Date Line. At midnight, it approached the line where the time on the other side was already June 6. With the crossing, the time changed to June 7, thus the Heywood records never showed June 6, 1944, D-Day.

Young's ship participated in the Leyte Gulf and Lingayon Gulf landings in the Philippines and the recapture of Okinawa. Earlier, it had participated in wave assaults on Attu and Kiska in the Aleutians, Guadalcanal, Tarawa (where Young's first wave Amtrac was destroyed fifty yards from the beach), and Kwajalein and Eniwetok in the Marshall Islands. Soon after VJ-day, Young had the honor of sailing the *Heywood* up Tokyo Bay as its navigator.

On Memorial Day, May 3, 1999, the *Greenville Herald Banner* ran a feature article on James Young and Gene Bench, who met quite by accident in the Greenville Wal-Mart Super Store. The article reported that Young, eighty-four, and Bench, seventy-two, were both wearing their t-shirts with the words "USS Heywood APA-6," which lists the landings the ship made during the war (Guadalcanal, Saipan, Okinawa, and Tokyo Bay) underneath the ship's name.

The men had known each other on the ship but had not had contact since 1945—over fifty-four years! The article related that Young had served as lieutenant on the *Heywood* for about three years, from February 1942 until he was discharged in December 1945. He had previously received his navigator's training at Notre Dame.

After he left the Navy, he attended Indiana University as a finance major working toward his doctorate. In 1947, his wife, two children, and he moved to Louisiana, where he was hired as full-time teacher at Louisiana State University. His career eventually led him to Dallas, where he worked for Grande National Life Insurance Company, then to Pennsylvania. He served as director of publications for the Wharton School of Finance. He took the director position when the incentive was given that in view of Young's wife being seriously ill with cancer, the area had the best radiation facilities in the United States.

In 1952, his wife died and he moved back to Dallas to continue working for Rio Grande. In 1966, he became a professor for East Texas State University in Commerce, Texas.

Young had his USS *Heywood* t-shirt made about six months before running into Mr. Bench at Wal-Mart. He said that almost every time he wore it anywhere, he ran into someone who had some connection with the war in the Pacific. When he spotted Bench with the same shirt, he walked up to him and asked if he had served on that ship. A conversation ensued, and they agreed to contact each other for more reminiscing.

In 1981, Young originated the first reunion of shipmates from the *Heywood*, and they continue to meet each year.

Jim Young, 1994
Tyler Rose Garden
Tyler, Texas

Lucy Wilson Jopling, 1942.

Lucy Wilson Jopling

Red Cross Nurse—Bataan and Corregidor
801st Medical Air Evacuation Squadron of 13th Air Force
Capt., Final Rank

When Army Lt. Lucy Iris Wilson arrived back home in Big Sandy, Texas, on July 19, 1942, hundreds of people were on hand to welcome her. They were eager to hear of her experiences as an Army nurse on Bataan peninsula in the Philippines during the early months of the war.

After graduating from Big Sandy High School, Lucy Wilson trained at Parkland Hospital in Dallas, Texas, and went to work in Tyler, Texas In 1940, a young nurse with a yen for adventure, she signed up to become a Red Cross nurse. A year later, she was nursing at an Army hospital near Manila in the Philippines when the Japanese attack on Pearl Harbor, on December 7, 1941, drew America into World War II.

Gen. Jonathan Wainwright surrendered the American troops in the Philippines in May 1942. Before that, Lucy was one of the 104 American nurses who cared for wounded soldiers in a jungle hospital on the Bataan peninsula. On April 8, 1942, she got only a few minutes' notice that she was being moved to the island of Corregidor before Bataan fell.

On that rock island, the nurses worked in a tunnel hospital until May 3, when they fled four days before the island was given up. Years later, she wrote a book, *Warrior in White,* that told the long-secret story of how she and eleven other nurses put out into the South China Sea in a small boat and were picked up by the U.S. submarine *Spearfish*. A harrowing twenty-two-day voyage through enemy-infested waters, with space and water short, brought them to safety in Fremantle, Australia. It was only then that her Big Sandy family learned that Lucy was not "missing in action" as they had been notified.

"Walking out in the middle of an operation with hundreds lined up under the trees, waiting for surgery, was devastating to me," she wrote in her book.

General Wainwright had dubbed the nurses "Angels of Bataan and Corregidor" for their service through bombing, strafing, sniping, sickness, and disease, living on a starvation diet, and working endless hours to care for their patients.

After a month-long voyage home on the USS *West Point,* Lieutenant Wilson was assigned to tour the nation, urging Americans to buy War Bonds and support the war effort. Her return home included a public reception in Gilmer, Texas, where she was filmed by Paramount News.

She was asked to write her story for William Holden, a movie star who was a public relations officer in the Air Corps, and Hank Greenberg, a baseball star, for a program at Will Rogers Auditorium in Fort Worth. This was broadcast on the "Wings in Swing" radio program on September 16, 1943.

As Red Cross nurses, Lucy and the others had "relative ranks." But when the Woman's Army Corps was given full status on July 1, 1943, the nurses were still trying to get commissions.

Lieutenant Wilson entered flight nurse school and qualified to fly in C-47s and C-54s that were used as ambulance planes. She asked to return to the Philippines, and in 1944 she sailed in a convoy to Noumea, New Caledonia, on the way to Espiritu Santos Island in New Hebrides. She was assigned chief nurse in the 801st Medical Air Evacuation Squadron of the 13th Air Force.

Lieutenant Wilson made combat flights into many Pacific islands, and in August 1944, she was awarded the Air Medal. By the time her service ended, Captain Wilson had received the Bronze Star and the Asiatic Pacific Campaign medal with eight bronze stars, among other decorations.

Her wedding plans with a young soldier whom she had met when they were both stationed at Fort Bliss, Texas, Dan Jopling, had been cut short when he was captured by the Japanese and endured the Bataan Death March. At the war's end, she heard that he had survived forty-two months of imprisonment by the Japanese in both Japan and Korea. In November 1945, she received a telegram and went to see the young officer at Bruns General Hospital in Santa Fe, New Mexico.

They were married on December 5, 1945. The physical ravages they both experienced followed them into peacetime, but they resolved to put the horrors of war behind them and raise their two sons and two daughters. Dan stayed in the Army, retiring as a lieutenant colonel in 1962. He became a Red Cross manager in Lawton, Oklahoma.

Lucy went back to nursing. When the family moved to New Mexico, Dan's home, she became a nurse at the Gallup Indian Medical Center. In 1975, they moved back to San Antonio, Texas, where she worked at the Brooke Army Medical Center and Randolph Air Force Base.

Col. Dan Jopling died in July 1985. It was after then that Lucy decided to write her autobiography. One of her sons, who was in college, read about his parents in a book called *But Not in Shame*. He asked Lucy why she had never told her children about her wartime experiences. She said she wrote her book *Warrior in White* mainly for them.

She received another signal honor in 1993 when she was recommended as an alternate to sponsor the new amphibious warship, the USS *Bataan*, in the event that the principal sponsor, the ninety-four-year-old widow of Gen. Douglas MacArthur, was not able to carry out her duties. General MacArthur was evacuated from Bataan to Australia on March 12, 1942, vowing, "I shall return." That was almost two months before Lucy Wilson and the eleven other nurses fled to the submarine.

She was one of twelve military heroes, one for each month, featured in essays of the 1987 calendar put out by the USAA, a company that provides military insurance.

"One of the highlights of my life was assisting in the evacuation of our POW's from Luzon, Philippines . . . the very same men I'd left there in May, 1942," Captain Joplin was quoted.

"Many times soldiers would walk up, touch my arm and say, 'I just want to touch you.'"

Noting that the "Angels" nurses endured heavy bombardments and were often just a step away from the fighting, the essay continued with the quotation, "I remember once in Corregidor, the Japanese landed a bomb right next to a group of soldiers. The noise brought me running out. There were bodies scattered all through there.

"Nichols Field near Fort McKinley was bombed right after Pearl Harbor. I was so scared that I

Lucy Wilson Jopling, 2000

was almost nauseated. That's when I learned that training is so important. I was the only nurse on duty in the surgical wards that night and I was terrified. I automatically did what I was trained for in an emergency."

Capt. Lucy Jopling died on Christmas Day, December 25, 2000.

About the Author

MILLIE JEAN COPPEDGE grew up on a farm in a small East Texas town. She attended East Texas State University, where she received her master's degree in Elementary Education, then went on to be certified in English as a Second Language. She has taught seventeen years for the Dallas Independent School District and is currently also teaching two writing courses at Eastfield College, Mesquite, Texas. She pursues her interests in World War II and family research, travel, and dance.

www.ingramcontent.com/pod-product-compliance
Lightning Source LLC
Chambersburg PA
CBHW060045100426
42742CB00014B/2710